# OVERCOMING MEDIOCRITY

## STRONG WOMEN

# OVERCOMING
# *Mediocrity*©

**A unique collection of stories from strong women
who have created their own lives of significance!**

Presented by Christie L. Ruffino

## DPWN Publishing

www.dpwnpublishing.com

For more information, contact:
DPWN Publishing
A division of the Dynamic Professional Women's Network, Inc.
1879 N. Neltnor Blvd. #316, West Chicago, IL 60185
www.dpwnpublishing.com
www.ourdpwn.com

Printed in the United States of America

ISBN: 978-1-939794-02-4

# Dedication

To every woman who does not believe she can make a difference and to every woman who believes she can move a mountain.

To every woman who continually makes sacrifices for those she loves and to every woman who prioritizes those moments when she can pamper and take care of her own needs.

To every woman who believes that she should settle for the life she has and to every woman who has overcome great odds to create her own life of significance.

To the strong women in this book who have shared their stories with you in hopes that their lessons of pain will become your lessons of power.

To the women in my life who believe I am significant and whom I believe are priceless.

# The Power of a Story

There is nothing more important in this world than the relationships we build and the legacy we leave in the lives of those who have crossed paths with us on our journey of life. It's the experiences we have along this journey that defines our individual uniqueness and creates our own powerful personal blueprint or our unique story snowflake.

It is this blueprint that can empower us to possess a distinct advantage over every other person in this world if leveraged correctly and shared. If we don't have the courage to share our snowflake, it will be lost forever. No one will have the same story and no one can repeat your story. Therefore, if you don't share your story, those who come after you will never learn anything from what you experienced and what you learned.

I feel that the most significant thing that we can do to add value back into this world is to master the narrative of our lives and share it. All of our leadership and moneymaking ability rests in our ability to discover, craft and deliver our personal story or message in a way that will that allow people to connect to us. The right story shared at the right time with the right person, can alter the trajectory of their life.

But, the most powerful aspect of a story is that we all have the ability to learn from other people's stories and then change the direction of the stories we are living to shape our ultimate destinies.

Power to you and the story of your life!

# Introduction

Welcome to our third in a series of anthology books that are intended to provide women with a platform to share their stories of encouragement, inspiration and prosperity. Our first book, Overcoming Mediocrity — Dynamic Edition, was a smashing success and was released in May of 2013 with 22 participating authors sharing their stories meant to inspire other women to succeed. In addition, we achieved bestselling status on Amazon in the motivational genre category in only one day. We then duplicated that success with our second Overcoming Mediocrity — Courageous Women book launched in April of 2014 with a subsequent bestselling status achievement.

My goal with this project initially was to build a strong brand and provide the women of my organization, The Dynamic Professional Women's Network, Inc., with a platform to share their stories. They would then be able to leverage their new author status to gain additional exposure for their business and greater blessings as they collaborate with the other authors as they share their stories with a wider audience. It has, however, taken on a life of its own and has made a bigger impact than anticipated as I hear testimonials from women who read the book and connected with one or more of the inspirational stories inside.

Because of this initial overwhelming success, I decided to develop a new vision for this venture which is much larger than the previous one. My new "Exciting, Magical and Wildly Epic Goal" for this project is to build a stronger brand for *Overcoming Mediocrity* and to have our collection of books become nationally recognized and carried by the big book stores in addition to our current Amazon distribution. I want the authors of the current, past and future volumes to gain increased exposure and greater blessings for aligning themselves with this project so they can share their stories with larger audiences and make a greater impact. (The Chicken Soup series did it, why can't we?)

It is with great honor and pride that I am able to share with you the stories from the courageous women on the following pages of this book, which is the third anthology book in this series. I have had the pleasure of getting to know each of these ladies to learn a little about whom they are and about the courageous stories they planned to share. I am also deeply inspired by the courage that they are still exhibiting by sharing the personal details of their lives with the sole intention of equipping the reader to learn from their experiences and to spare themselves a little pain, if possible. Not only does this demonstrate courage, but it also shows the humility and heart of a true go-giver. These women, while still on the amazing journey of their lives, all have great things yet to come. They are women who you should know, learn from and emulate.

I am blessed to have had that opportunity.

Christie

# Table of Contents

Christie Lee Ruffino: Overcoming Fear with a Giant Leap of Faith ...... 1

Dr. Kris Sargent: It Doesn't Happen by Accident ................................. 11

Laurie A. Polinski: Feeding the Fire: Finding Your True You .............. 19

Dr. Ingryd Lorenzana: Hold Fast to the Sacred Sparks Inside You ..... 27

Starla Snead: The Serenity Prayer—Many Lessons in Authenticity..... 35

Susan M. Sparks: The Riches in a Rag-Tag Resume............................. 43

Ursula Wachowiak: How The B.R.O.A.D. was Born and Reborn ........ 51

Dori J. Mages: 12 Attributes Strong Women Need for Success ........... 61

Dede Schwartz: Determined To Achieve ............................................... 71

Debra Sunderland: It is All in What You Tell Yourself........................ 81

Valerie Janke: Finding Balance through Strength ............................... 91

Dr. Emily Loveland: Make Wellness Your Reality................................. 99

Michele Saxman: The Secret .............................................................. 105

Kim Brondyke: My Journey to Become an Empowered Survivor ..... 113

Noël Thelander: What's in Your Back Pocket?................................... 121

Noel Baldwin: I Can't Wait to See What's Next ................................ 131

Jordan Holwell: Me Strong? ............................................................. 139

Sabrina Swanson: Dreaming in Color ............................................... 147

Carol O'Meara: Explore and Dream to Discover Your Strengths: An Australian Story.............................................................................. 153

# Christie Lee Ruffino

## *Overcoming Fear with a Giant Leap of Faith*

I remember being so terrified that I was shaking uncontrollably. My voice cracked as I was finally able to utter recognizable words through my endless stream of sobs. Yet I was also a bit excited and deeply calm at the thought of what was to come next in my life. It was as if I were standing on the edge of an open plane door, looking at the beautiful skies and endless world below, anticipating the adrenaline rush and terrifying fear of stepping out into thin air and freefalling 13,000 feet, safely back down to Earth.

Yet, I wasn't skydiving. I was taking a giant leap of faith in making a difficult decision to leave a secure and well-paying job that just didn't fit. Why the tears and fears? I was a newly divorced mom, trying to make my way in an industry that left me drained and unhappy. Despite the well-meaning advice of others to stay put, I had faith and a drive to embark on a different journey that overshadowed the reality of bills and obligations. I wanted to make a more significant impact in the world and utilize the gifts that God blessed me with. Was it a risk? Without a doubt. But it is true that, "with great risk comes great reward".

The only other time in my life when I had similar feelings was when I was 21, standing at the altar, about to be married to my high-school sweetheart. I was so excited to be living out every girl's Disney fairytale wedding. I primped and prepared for months to be the beautiful bride in a spectacular dress, with a church full of family and friends and the possibility of living happily ever after with my Prince Charming. It was all very overwhelming for me, yet I was very happy that the day had finally come. At the same time, I was completely terrified. Should I get married? Should I be marrying this man? Will I be a good wife? Will things be better in our relationship now that we are husband and wife? Will the cake be delivered on time for the reception? Will Uncle Bob cause a scene tonight after a few too many cocktails? And boy, am I hot in this long sleeve wedding dress in mid-July in a non-air conditioned, 90 degree church? What was I thinking?

This time, however, I was not getting married. I was standing in my boss's office trembling to the core, scared out of my mind and riddled with guilt, as I was about to tell her "I quit".

I wasn't quitting because I didn't like to work. I really love working; especially when the job allows me the opportunity to learn and accomplish something worthwhile. I've had one or more jobs at a time since I was 15. Some were short gigs, but most of the jobs I had lasted for years because I am a loyal and dedicated worker. If the jobs were boring, I became more engaged and found various ways to make the job better and provide additional support for my employer. I created additional duties and stepped into higher roles as they became available. I was the ideal employee!

Such was the case with the boss I was standing in front of now. She hired me based on a referral from a friend at church who also worked there. I was hired as a loan processor at a mortgage company even though I knew nothing about the industry. I had a lot of experience at marketing and managing the finances for our small auto repair business, but my resume was sparse and I knew nothing about mortgages and interest rates. But this was a good company that was owned and managed by Christian people who wanted to help me get on my feet due to my newly divorced status. I learned the processing duties and worked well with the loan officers and their clients to ensure that their loan packages were complete and their closings were successful. The people I worked with were wonderful to me. They were like my new family and I felt very blessed to be earning a living at a job that I enjoyed.

I quickly transitioned from the processing position to loan officer because the duties were more aligned with my skills. Even better, I would be able to make a higher income based on my efforts. So I poured myself into my new commission-based role to help people with their mortgage needs. But there was something that started to stir around in my gut that didn't feel right. I was just not sure yet what it was.

However, I became fully committed to succeeding with this new position. Since my pay structure was mostly based on sales commissions, I had to get out and start generating my own new business. I began networking like a crazy woman to find people who were shopping for a new house or wanted a better interest rate on their existing mortgage. While I was super busy, I was just not getting the results I needed to pay my bills. I needed to make more progress and make it faster. It was at this time that I was invited to attend my first referral group meeting. What a great idea, I thought, since my product was of such a personal nature it made sense for me to become involved with an industry exclusive group that focused on building relationships with other professionals who would refer me business as one of their trusted referral partners. It was perfect!

The only problem now was that since the industry was so saturated with loan officers, I was not able to find a local group with my business category open. I didn't give up. Through a series of events and introductions, I became part of a brand new, independent group that allowed me to selectively invite other women to join based on the business they represented and the level of professionalism that they dedicated to manage their business. I could assemble my own trusted referral team. What could be better than that?

**The DPWN Story Begins…**

That initial group only lasted a few months, but the seed was planted for what today is the Dynamic Professional Women's Network. The organizer stepped down from that group and since I had already become committed to our little network, I decided to continue with the plan under our own name, the DuPage Professional Women's Network. I researched the structures and policies of other well-known referral groups in the industry and came up with what I thought was the best of them to form the initial foundation of DPWN. Our biggest variation from the other national referral organizations is that I wanted our group to be exclusively female because it created a unique dynamic that differed from co-ed groups. It was not a matter of a women's group being better in any way. However, I wanted to capitalize on the powerful camaraderie and energy that women can develop together. I also knew that some of the policies from the other groups could be improved upon to be more conducive to our target member, the working mom. I wanted to be structured and productive, yet we still needed to keep our family obligations a priority. Over time, with the help of my newly formed leadership team, we defined and refined the policies, structures, and benefits of membership to make our organization the strongest and most relevant resource for professional women out there.

That initial chapter became a very productive and successful networking community. We eventually had a waiting list of women who wanted to join, but were unable to because either their business category was already occupied, or the chapter had reached its capacity. It was a great problem to have after working so hard to achieve our success, yet I felt guilty for turning away so many women. Then during a leadership planning meeting, one of the members suggested that we launch a second chapter a few towns away. She volunteered to run it because it would be closer to her business. What a great idea, I thought! And that was the beginning of our expansion that has continued to evolve into additional chapters throughout the Chicagoland suburbs, the city of Chicago, and even into other states.

**Are You Living Your Life of Significance?**

Since the late 1990s, Gallup (www.gallup.com), the Washington, D.C.-based polling organization, has been measuring international employee satisfaction through a survey it has been honing over the years. Their latest findings indicate that only 30% of workers actually feel engaged by their jobs. That means that a whole 70% are "not engaged", are emotionally disconnected or do not experience a sense of passion for their work. It was a statistic that I just did not want to become. I could feel myself slipping into that segment and I did not like it.

Working in the mortgage industry, did allow me to use bits and pieces of my marketing skills, but the paperwork, number crunching, and the endless hours of research to find the best loan product for each client was making me feel drained and unhappy. Yes, I was earning a living and supporting my children, but I knew deep down that being in the loan industry was not what God had planned for me and my life. My talents were not being utilized and I was not able to pursue my passions, even though I really was not completely sure what my passions were yet. But I was starting to think that it was about time for me to begin figuring that out.

I had many questions swirling around in my head. Because I was very new to my faith, I was uncertain if my feelings and thoughts of quitting were God-inspired or Christie-inspired? And if they were God inspired, I did not understand why He would want me to leave my only means of financial income without a plan B? I wondered if I was being selfish to want to work in a job that would really make me happy. The general consensus from my family and friends, including myself at times, was that I was Crazy with a capital C for even considering to quit my job. But after some pretty heavy soul searching, I took a leap of faith and knocked on my boss's door to resign from their wonderful company.

When I made up my mind to leave the mortgage company, I only had one chapter of DPWN, and chapter expansion had never even crossed my mind let alone the concept of building a national networking organization. But I learned so much about myself during these transitional years that I knew it was time for me to begin making decisions that were right for ME and would allow me to utilize the gifts that God had blessed me with.

## So the Search Continues...

I eventually landed my next job in the employment industry. I loved this job because I was helping employers find the right talent for their needs while helping other job seekers like myself find great jobs. The best aspect, however, was that I was able to remain connected to my networking group and to utilize the relationships I had formed to quickly build a thriving client base in this new job. Once again, I was the ideal employee!

After two years of building my employment business and running that first large and very productive DuPage chapter, I was ready to take another step into my DPWN future. I still did not know that this one step would lead to more, but in 2007 I made a decision to launch a second DPWN chapter in a neighboring town because I had a strong member willing to lead it. It was hard to stop after that. Once the word got out that we had a second chapter, women began contacting me about launching a chapter in their own town and we had chapters popping up in areas other than DuPage County. It was incredible! We began expanding simply though organic word-of-mouth referrals from our existing members. They were getting results and they wanted to share it with other professional women whom they respected. It was at this time, that I made things official. I incorporated the organization and changed its name to the Dynamic Professional Women's Network, Inc. (DPWN), and continued to juggle its growth while still maintaining my position at the employment agency. Things were a bit crazy!

I was eventually faced with another decision and was once again, standing in my new boss's office, trembling to the core, scared out of my mind and riddled with guilt, telling him "I quit". I liked this job and I liked the freedom my boss gave me to build his business. However, I was investing more and more time into DPWN and discovered that I really *loved* it. I did it. I finally figured out what I wanted to do. I was feeling completely satisfied with the results that I was getting to help women build their businesses in our organization. I just had to continue building it to the point that it could now support me and my family while still providing enough capital to invest back into its organizational growth.

**Fast Forward to Today.**

Through the collective effort of the amazing women throughout the years who have taken on leadership roles, we have created the BEST industry-exclusive networking organization around. It is designed to help women create partnerships with each other to generate ideas, alliances, and revenues within a structured referral generating format. Since that first spin off chapter was launched in 2007, more than 1600 members have joined DPWN, recognizing it as a driving force behind the success and profitability for many of our members' businesses. We are just getting started. We plan to quadruple that number in the next few years and become a national organization for women that will provide much more than an opportunity to network. We expect to be a complete resource for their professional development and marketing needs.

I also launched a new publishing division of the organization as a resource for our members to leverage their status as authors and gain increased exposure and credibility for their businesses by participating in one of our *Overcoming Mediocrity* anthology books, or by publishing their own solo-books. Books are the new business card, and my goal with this project is to provide an easy and affordable way for my members to take advantage of this powerful marketing tool.

My overall objective is to help more women cash in on their unique strengths by offering them a process to easily discover, craft, and deliver their personal story or message in a way that builds immediate intimacy, trust, and loyalty. There are many ways to do this; from crafting a powerful 30 second elevator speech, and/or delivering the best signature speech to the ideal client or audience, to writing a book that will offer value to the reader and provides instant credibility, recognition, respect, and endless exposure and marketing benefits. There is so much we can do as we work together and empower each other.

**Are You Ready to Leap too?**

Perhaps you have stood where I was that initial day, shaking in your shoes, ready to declare your independence, and to begin a new adventure. Maybe you are working hard in a career, yet have a gut feeling that something just isn't right and think you can only dream of making that leap of faith. Look around, there are women just like you who have done it and they are willing to help you do it too.

The joy and satisfaction of building DPWN is reinforced to me daily, as I hear of women who have made great connections, exchanged ideas, and grown personally and professionally. It is my hope that you recognize those around you who have been put in your path to help you realize your dream and that you listen to the promptings of God.

Both times I made the decision to leave my job, people called me crazy. However, they were the most empowering moves I have ever made. God was using various people and circumstances to provide me direction along the way, I only had to listen. I had to be willing to overcome my fears, and to take that leap of faith. Now, I wake up every day thankful for that shaky moment: the tears, the fears, and the leap to my perfect landing. I finally discovered MY answer to the question: What do you want to be when you grow up? I completely believe that you may not always end up where you thought you were going, but if you listen to God, you will always end up where you are meant to be.

# Christie Lee Ruffino

As the President and Founder of the Dynamic Professional Women's Network, Inc., Christie Ruffino is passionate about empowering and equipping women to create significant lives regardless of the challenges that they face along the way. Because of the many women who have built thriving businesses in her community, Christie has been dedicated to the continual evolution of the company ensuring that new benefits and opportunities are provided to her members each year.

The Dynamic Professional Women's Network, Inc. (DPWN), is an industry exclusive networking organization designed to help women create partnerships with each other to generate ideas, alliances, and revenues within a structured referral generating format. There are referral chapters in many states, and each chapter has only one member from any business category. Since its conception, more than 1600 members have joined DPWN, recognizing it as a driving force behind the success and profitability of many of its members' businesses.

In addition to working diligently to ensure the success of the Dynamic Professional Women's Network and the DPWN Angel Foundation, Ms. Ruffino is a past Council Member of the Executives Breakfast Club, served two terms as a Board Director of the Carol Stream Chamber of Commerce, received a 2008 Special Judge's Recognition for the Citizen of the Year award in Carol Stream, in 2009 was awarded a Distinguished Woman of Business Award from American Family Insurance with great pleasure and received her highest honor by being recognized as an Influential Women in Business in 2009 by the Business Ledger and the National Association of Women Business Owners (NAWBO) and in 2010 with an Entrepreneurial Excellence Award.

Christie is now dedicated to helping others cash in on their unique strengths by offering them a process to easily discover, craft and deliver their personal story or message in a way that will build immediate intimacy, trust and loyalty with her "Personal Power Story Action Program".

Christie Lee Ruffino
Dynamic Professional Women's Network, Inc.
1879 N. Neltnor Blvd. #316
West Chicago, IL 60185
630-336-3773
info@ourdpwn.com
www.OurDPWN.com
www.ChristieRuffino.com

# Dr. Kris Sargent
## *It Doesn't Happen by Accident*

The last several years have served as an awakening, of sorts, in my world. I have faced trials and triumphs in that time that I never dreamed would be part of my life. I grew up knowing the basics of success philosophy. At a very early age, I was exposed to the great thought leaders of the past like Zig Ziglar, Jim Rohn, Dale Carnegie and Napoleon Hill. These gentlemen knew age-old truths and were able to communicate them in unique ways. My parents knew these were important lessons to be taught, and I learned them well. My mom even had a little box, with a slit carved into the top, on the hearth. Written on it was "25 cents". It was the "Can't" box. We had to pay if we said "I can't do…" She was serious about us believing we could achieve anything! If we could see it, and believe it, we could achieve it! But someplace along my journey, the world knocked that out of me and my dreams were shattered.

I have always known one thing. I believe there is a God, a Higher Power, an angel or the Universe looking out for me. Call it what you want. I have always had a strong faith that whatever circumstance was put in my life, it was put there to teach me something. Incidents in my life steered me to being reconnected to my core principles, and now I am in the fortunate position to share some of what I have learned. I sincerely hope that you will take what I am about to share to heart. If you don't agree with something, that is fine, leave it on the page and take what applies for you. I think you will see that most of the principles are inextricably linked.

**Possibilities, Fear, Options and Choices.**

As a gift or a curse, in almost every relationship and circumstance around me, I have learned to see the positive potential and possibilities. This is a trait of an eternal optimist and can be very annoying to friends and family members who are looking for a sympathetic ear to their plight. The key I learned is that in any given situation or circumstance, there are always more options and choices than we initially recognize. It's bigger than making lemonade out of lemons. It's realizing you actually have an opportunity to make fruit punch! The fact is, we tend to see life in a black and white mode. Finding a new set of lenses or sometimes just realizing you need new lenses can be all it takes to shift your sights to the unseen possibilities. What keeps you from seeing this potential?

Fear. Fear! The big liar! Fear is our emotion of survival. It arises from the part of the brain known as the amygdala and is designed to keep us out of life threatening trouble. Interestingly, in our society, the things that are most life threatening, too much junk food and a sedentary lifestyle, don't exactly appear life threatening to the amygdala. One of my mentors taught me that fear speeds you up. Your heart pounds in your chest, breathing rate increases, you move and think too fast when you are coming from a place of fear. Fear can also paralyze you to the point where you are stuck. It can bring you to a point where you believe there aren't any options.

In that moment, you can become the queen (or King) of your emotions and thoughts. You can choose whether to react or respond. Yes, I found this a huge challenge to my self-awareness. Try this, imagine you are sitting on your throne, and all of your "town's people" are seated below you. But, they are not really "town's people", they are your emotions and thoughts. One by one you can listen, and chose what you want to hear and heed. Remember, you will always get what you think about the most. When the freak out moments arise, and they will, you can assess the fear for its authenticity. You can chose to stare it down. Look right at it and name it! Then, you can choose to overcome it. It is up to us to keep our amygdala, our "town's people," straight about what is reality.

Practically speaking, it is important to possess new skills to be able to listen to your "town's people". Several successful strategies I have uncovered include:

1. Deep diaphragmatic breathing reduces stress hormones, just breathe then listen

2. Journaling allows feelings and thoughts to flow onto paper

3. Talking to a friend or trusted advisor

4. Meditating, praying, yoga, find a quiet place

5. Expressing yourself through art, music or dance

6. Walking or any other form of exercise increases blood flow and oxygen to the brain

7. Positive books by authors such as Darren Hardy, Robert Holden, Napoleon Hill and Dale Carnegie

8. Uplifting music

9. Find gratitude every day, anxiety can't live in gratitude

With practice, you will discover which tactic(s) work best for you. Your newly found emotional intelligence will bring you to a more neutral perspective, shift your brain into a creative space to form new options, solutions, possibilities and choices for your life. Then, you can make a powerful response.

**Eat, Drink, Move and Think.**

Take care of yourself. How many times have you heard that? And how many times have you agreed with that? And how many times have you come up with an excuse for why you can't take care of yourself? Is there a fear of selfishness that takes over? Although this has been part of my life's work, there was a time when I wasn't listening either. In an instant, I made a choice to look for a different set of options and you can too.

I woke up 5 years after Cooper was born, 40 pounds overweight and huffing as I climbed the stairs. I had always been in shape but with a little weight challenge. This was out of hand. My kids were little and I was an "older" mom. I wanted to be super healthy for them as a role model. It was time to take my own advice. I asked myself a few questions. What time could I create to get to the gym? I wasn't typically a morning person, but I knew in order to accomplish my goal, morning workouts were my best opportunity. Hiring a trainer kept me accountable and taught me a new way to move. I was brutally honest with myself about what I was eating through a food log. Poor food choices didn't fly into my mouth on their own, it was a choice! I was in charge of the fork. I took off 45 pounds and left the lean muscle mass. My Eat for Energy plan is available for you on my website.

You have the power to remake your body, even over 40 or at any age. You can learn how to fit self-care around a busy lifestyle. Just know the possibility exists! It is a win-win. You will be happier and more successful in all of your roles.

**Exceptional "Be"**

Staying a healthy weight and taking care of yourself is just part of a full life. We all aspire to being exceptional, to making a difference and becoming significant. We constantly look for the magic wand or the supernatural formula that will bring us to that goal, without too much introspection or work. We think we have to HAVE something in order to DO something so we can BE something. Right? It goes like this, if I just HAD more money, then I could DO such and such, then I would BE successful. The truth is that looking for the "have" or the "do" is actually backwards to how you can BE the best version of you. When we look outside of ourselves for the magic formula we are no longer trusting that we were made with all the tools necessary to succeed.

I can tell you without a doubt, you were made perfect from the beginning. Yes, I had many painful lessons to get to the point where I actually believed that statement. I couldn't wrap my head around it for the longest time. I kept trying to do, do, do and felt like I was banging my head against a wall. Then I remembered something from my childhood. We are made in the image of

God, our Higher Power and the Universe. That is a perfect image. We may not always ACT perfect or make perfect decisions, but that doesn't take away from our design. This also means that you possess all the knowledge you need to be the best version of you possible!

To begin to get in touch with that perfection inside you, learn what makes you tick. First, your intuition can be found when you are listening to your "town's people". Once you begin to hear your emotions and thoughts clearly, you will feel those emotions in your belly, or your heart and your throat. Take note of the location and what it is telling you. Put it into words. This is your intuition, it is your heart or gut. The process of trusting yourself is the beginning. Second, is understanding your value system.

Next, get a clear view of your value system. To help you, I have a short values assessment available for you online. My top values are Responsibility, Courage, Discipline, Health, Spirituality, Family and Integrity/Continuity. When I am faced with making a choice, I run the possibilities, choices and options through my value system, my intuition and listen to my emotions. I ask myself if I am within my values before I make any decision. In this way, you will not stray from what is important in your life.

It's in this self-trust of intuition and continuity to your own values that you will shine. You will begin to "BE" different, to show up in the world differently. You will have a new sense of self confidence in knowing you are being who you were intended to be. The be, do, and have of life is now in the proper order. Taking time to unearth what is important to you and what turns you on, will shed light on the perfection that is you! Once you have chosen to BE that best version of you, you will start doing things differently, and you will have your hearts desires.

**Never Give Up.**

I was joking with a friend that my middle names are Perseverance and Endurance, yes, long names! Pun intended. Never give up. There is always another day. Never give up. There is always another way. Trust and faith go the distance to help you maintain hope that you can make it through any situation. Shifting your thought patterns will help you stay in the game and not give up when you think you can't move forward. The same strategies you use for moving past fear can be employed when you feel like giving up. Kelly Clarkson sings it best, "What doesn't kill you makes you stronger." Another current favorite is by Nickelback called "What are You Waiting for?" My playlist is full of songs I listen to when I feel like giving up.

Don't just let your life happen to you. As I said in the beginning, I let the world smother my dreams. I also knew there had to be a different way to look at life. I wish I could tell you I had it all figured out. I know there are more lessons I will learn on this journey. But I always know, the expanse of the universe is essentially unlimited, so are the possibilities for life. Become the designer of your life. It's not paint by numbers with the colors assigned to a particular picture. You can have a fresh canvas any moment of any day. See the possibilities. An amazing life doesn't happen by accident and some of the most outlandish ideas will lead to some of your greatest successes.

# Dr. Kris Sargent

Dr. Kris Sargent is a cutting edge expert in Functional Medicine. She creates personalized solutions for fatigue, weight loss, hormone issues, sleep, achiness and digestive problems. She has numerous credentials that are listed below. She is most appreciative for are the poignant and sometimes painful life lessons her parents, children, ex-husband and coaches have pushed her to learn. They believed in her at times when she didn't believe in herself, until she finally realized that God only makes fabulous! Now she wants to share what she has learned from clinical practice, and life's ups and downs.

Dr. Sargent's interest in Functional Nutrition started with her desire to solve some of her own health issues. Her personal experience created a keen understanding of the need for using a patient's health history and current symptoms to format unique solutions. As a single mother, business owner and busy entrepreneur, she understands the importance of self-care for the strength and resilience necessary to positively move through the challenges of life. As a result, she is launching a series of books that will make the process of applying functional medicine to real life easy and fun. She put the "fun" in FUNctional Medicine. Eat, Drink, Move, Sleep and Think your way to health!

She graduated with degrees in Biology and Psychology from the University of Central Florida in 1988. Along with a BS in Human Anatomy, she completed her Doctorate of Chiropractic degree at The University of Health Sciences in 1992. Over the years, Dr. Sargent has accumulated hundreds of hours of continuing education in Functional Nutrition, Leadership and Personal Development, Certification in First Line Therapy, a post-doctoral Master's Degree in Advanced Clinical Practice, and 22 years in practice. Dr. Sargent considers herself to be a clinical science geek and sleuth.

Dr. Kris Sargent
Restor Healing Centre
416 E Roosevelt Road, Suite 107
Wheaton, IL 60187
630-682-5090
restorceo@gmail.com
www.RestorYou.com
www.TheGutsyGal.com

# Laurie A. Polinski

## *Feeding the Fire: Finding Your True You*

Do you know who you are?

"Silly question," you might answer, "I've spent 24 hours a day with myself for … 40-some years! I'm a wife, mom, accountant, volunteer, VP at XYZ Corporation." OK, but our roles don't define *who* we are. It goes much deeper than that.

Each of us is unique, with our own gifts, strengths and a "unique brilliance" or "inner fire" that is the essence of our authentic self. Inside each of us, there is a deep-seated longing to let this brilliance lead how to live our lives. If we neglect it, this inner fire will only fuel our search for a more enjoyable, fulfilling life. If we identify and nurture it, this inner fire will empower us to express our true essence and unleash the abundance that we receive from living authentically. Only then can we live joyfully, with purpose and direction.

Many of us struggle with questions like "Am I on the right path?" "What should I be doing? "Which direction should I go?" For me, it took years of discomfort and struggle within my own skin to become self-aware enough to realize all that I had to offer, and how intensely I wanted to offer it to the world. For me, a quiet, inner fire smoldering below the surface, was waiting for the chance to burn brightly, and illuminate my gifts and true purpose to the world.

Today, this inner fire fuels my passion and life's work as a transformational success coach, but first I had to increase my self-awareness. One of my greatest life lessons is that self-awareness unlocks the doors that lead to happiness and success.

## Having it All?

It took decades for me to finally understand myself, my own gifts, and my purpose. As a child, I remember having a sense of restlessness, as if I needed to do something more, but I didn't know what. I remember my mom noticing and asking why I was so dissatisfied all the time. Why was I always seeking something more?

My dissatisfaction compelled me to succeed. I sought fulfillment through training, education and changing jobs until I eventually landed a job at one of the most recognized companies in the world, the McDonald's Corporation. Even with this incredible accomplishment, I still had this deep inner sense that there was something more. I was hoping that someone at the company or outside myself would notice something in me and point me in the right direction, but it didn't happen. Instead, I worked harder, built a loving family life, lived in a nice home and continued to deal with the nagging, discomforting, and truly distressing feeling within.

What was wrong with me? To the outward eye, I "had it all"— loving husband, children, great career—so why did I have this sense of restlessness?

Change became a short-term distraction from the inner sense of angst and dis-ease. I tried moving from home to home and immersing myself in home improvement projects to quell my feelings, but I still kept looking for... something. My husband even once joked that I had indeed seemed to change everything except for him and the kids! What was next?

At one time, I hired various life coaches to help me figure out what I needed. They tried to help me get from point A to point B. However, they couldn't help me identify the "Point B", which was precisely what I needed to do.

Over time, I began to wonder if maybe I was wrong. Maybe my passion and my search didn't have a deeper purpose. Yet, how could I deny these feelings that relentlessly pushed me to look around every corner, turn over every stone to find that missing "something?" I threw myself into the study of human potential, metaphysics, spirituality, and personal development, but it wasn't there. Sometimes frustrated to tears, I just wished someone could lead me to my inner passion, and point me in the right direction so that I could just get on with it!

I shared my frustrations with my friend, Debbie. She suggested that I look into a personality assessment called CORE MAP®. I was skeptical. In the corporate world, I had taken many personality assessments with the same results. I was a "reserved, introverted nurturer who thrives on details." Debbie insisted that CORE MAP was different. CORE MAP would show me where I was getting in my own way, point out blind spots I may have about myself, and give me specific direction to move forward.

I took the assessment. Soon, I was sitting in a small room across from a life coach who was about to give me information that would forever change the way I perceived myself. That day I learned that I didn't have to be the "reserved, introverted nurturer that thrives on details" from the personality assessments of the past. I learned that my true innate traits, strengths and passions were radically different. I was shown to be creative and intuitive, and someone who thrives on creating change in the world.

Suddenly, my search for "something more" made perfect sense. That "something" was within me the whole time. It wasn't another job, home-improvement project or workshop. It was my untapped, dormant potential that was waiting to emerge from within and lead me down my right path. I felt like someone had just handed me the Willy Wonka Golden Ticket to my life and said, "Here, you're free to be you."

I realized that for so long, I had been on the wrong path heading in the wrong direction. My innate gifts and strengths had been unrealized, so it was natural to feel restless, dissatisfied, and discouraged. I had created a beautiful life that I wouldn't change for the world, but I wasn't fully living, since I was completely unaware of everything I had and could offer to the world.

Joyously, this new self-awareness gave me permission to seek out and embrace different options in life. I explored aspects of myself that had been buried since childhood. I gained an incredible new level of confidence and appreciation for who I am. I tried new things and pursued leadership roles that I would never have before. New doors of possibilities opened for me everywhere that I turned.

I could now see my inner fire and understand the power it gave me to claim the life I was meant to live. Here I was standing before a once smoldering flame, but now I was fanning it and the energy was rising. I was pointed in the right direction and knew that my "Point B" was closer than ever!

Finally, after a life of looking for "something more," I was compelled to choose another path, my path. Only, instead of hoping it would lead me somewhere, I was confident where I was going, as I was led by my innate gifts and strengths. I now understood why I could not live authentically in my corporate position. With confidence, I took a deep breath and made the decision to leave my job.

**Life as the True Me**

I could never have found my right path without this new self-awareness of my authentic self. I took the skills and training that I'd acquired over my years in the corporate world, and started my own business. I helped small businesses build a strong brand identity so that they could grow their business, attract more clients and do more of what they loved to do. In this way, I began to stoke that inner fire which was now an empowering engine, driving me forward.

The creativity that I once channeled into random home improvement projects was now expressed in my work with clients. Best of all, the more that I tapped into these new passions and skills, the more alive they became. Even more gifts and strengths, like my strong intuitive sense and leadership skills, began to reveal themselves.

I was now fully ignited from within, using my gifts with purpose and direction. I was adding fuel to that internal flame. My intuition astounded my clients, and me as well. They would wonder how I came up with such perceptive suggestions and I realized I surely had had these natural gifts all along. Yet, without awareness, they laid dormant. My business grew with happy, successful clients and I loved my work more than I ever imagined possible. However, the most rewarding result, after years of wondering and searching, was that my "point B" finally revealed itself.

**Point B at Last**

Even as I coached scores of business leaders to achieve their bottom line goals, I discovered my inner fire blazes most brightly when I help individuals do what I did—discover their own unique strengths and set out on the right path to achieve their full potential. I use my innate gifts of intuition, creativity and big-picture thinking to unleash their brilliance and guide them in the right direction. This is what truly gives me intense satisfaction, and a feeling of complete fulfillment and confidence that I am living my life with purpose, direction and in service to the greater good.

When restless people come to me on a search for their own "Point B," I now have the tools and knowledge to help them side-step the long, painful journey I had to take. I show them how to discover their own gifts and live authentically to experience greater self-empowerment, more rewarding relationships, and open the doors to success.

Today, I am more self-aware, self-confident, and at peace with who I am than I ever thought possible. I am also living proof that before you can find your "Point B," you must increase your level of self-awareness, which is essential to determining where that inner fire can take you.

So what's burning inside of you? Is your inner fire yearning to be ignited?

Here are some sure-fire steps, based on my program, "Clarity, Purpose, and Prosperity," to set that inner fire ablaze!

**Step One: CLARITY — Discover your authentic self. Uncover your greatest gifts, strengths, and passions.** There are many tools available to help you do this, including the CORE MAP®. A life coach can also lead you to self-discovery. The right questions, tools and techniques can help you uncover who you were born to be, what you are here to do, and what fuels your passions. You will be surprised how quickly it can happen.

**Step Two: PURPOSE — Determine a Clarity of Purpose and Direction.** Your purpose allows you to open up to receive abundance into your life. To find your purpose, you must tap into and utilize your greatest gifts, strengths, and passions, while expanding to embrace something bigger than yourself. Then you can banish self-doubt and self-sabotaging blocks and barriers that stand in the way of your heart's desires. You will acquire a clear sense of direction. You will find inner confidence, peace of mind and the ability to make quicker decisions unencumbered by fears as your purpose flows through you.

**Step Three: PROSPERITY — Fueled by your purpose, you open yourself up to greater and greater abundance, opportunities and success.** At this stage, your life becomes fueled by your inner fire in accord with your authentic path. Your fire burns brightly and you become magnetically attractive to all that you want in life. New possibilities and opportunities begin to flow to you in unexpected ways and open the doors to prosperity, abundance, and success. You'll wake up every morning with the enthusiasm and motivation to live the life you want.

Remember, everything starts with self-awareness. Only then can we find the right path that will help us reach our highest potential and live our destiny. We all have gifts and a unique brilliance, but it is easy to leave them deeply buried within. By becoming more self-aware, we can find that inner fire and stoke it until it is blazing brilliantly for all to behold. You'll be surprised how living authentically ensures that you'll never be looking for "something" again!

# Laurie A. Polinski

As a personal transformation leader, Laurie Polinski is passionate about helping others find their own unique brilliance to experience greater meaning and fulfillment in their business, relationships, and personal life. Her foray into life coaching began after 20+ years at a Fortune 500 company, and her own personal search to find her true essence. Laurie founded Absolute Certainty in 2002, and helps individuals, including entrepreneurs and executives, unleash their potential for success by helping them to uncover their true strengths.

Recently, Laurie co-founded Courageous Leadership Coaching Academy (www.courageousleadershipcoach.com). The certification program develops life coaches with an emphasis on letting one's true purpose, rather than circumstances, determine life's path. Laurie herself holds multiple coaching certifications, making her a Certified Quantum Leap Coach, Certified Dream Coach, Certified Creating Abundance Coach, Certified Brainwave

Consultant, Certified CORE MAP® Facilitator, and Certified Integrative Freedom Technique Practitioner.

Laurie is a frequent guest on blog talk radio programs including "An Inside Job: Mastery Conversations" with Leah Young; Igniting the Peace Within with Mercedes Warrick and I Am Healthy Radio with Dr. James Joseph. She is a graduate of the Inspiring Speaker Program, studying under Dream University® founder, Marcia Wieder and co-host of Chicago's West Suburban Chapter of Engaging Speakers.

Laurie attended DePaul University and is a Board Member and Director of National Marketing for the non-profit organization LifeSigns, Inc., which equips women and veterans with resources for personal, professional and economic empowerment.

Laurie A. Polinski, CPC
Absolute Certainty Coaching
6930 Webster St
Downers Grove, IL 60516
630-881-6237
Laurie@LauriePolinski.com
www.LauriePolinski.com

# Dr. Ingryd Lorenzana
## *Hold Fast to the Sacred Sparks Inside You*

In Colombia, the end of every elementary school year ended with a *clausura,* a closing ceremony to celebrate another academic year accomplished. I remember these "assembly-like" ceremonies being a big deal. Children in every grade were filled with anticipation of their distinct grade performance, which was kept secret to the rest of the school until the actual Special Day. We would wear special outfits and celebrate. For me, the one clausura I remember most was my kindergarten year.

My mom, a single mother, and I lived with a family that she worked for as a second job. We shared a bedroom located near the kitchen and the patio with another lady who also worked for them. The host family's fourth child, a daughter close to my age, and I became friends. She was always very kind to me and would share her stuff with me. I remember her having more things than me and liking her room more than mine. However, I don't remember feeling any different than her because of it. My mom, however, whether intentionally or not, would say stuff that did make me feel different. She would say: "Don't touch her stuff," and "Stay out of her room." I hated the way her words made me feel. The evening of my kindergarten clausura, I was still wearing my special outfit that my mom had sewn for me, a red ruffled midrib silky shirt with some small white shorts. It was fitting for a *cumbia,* which had been my grade's dance. I remember getting in trouble with mom again because I had touched the little girl's doll. I remember once again hating the way her words made me feel, as though I was not *special* enough or maybe even that she loved the girl more than me.

However, I also remember knowing where I felt loved and who made me feel special. For me, that was my grandmother or abuelita. That night, filled with determination to feel special and make that horrible feeling inside go away, I decided that I had had enough. Close to midnight, while my mom was busy helping with the little girl's clausura party, I decided to go to my grandmother's house, about 20 miles away. I was only five years old but I do remember knowing that I wanted my *abuelita*. Even though it was dark outside, I was not afraid because I knew the way to her house. Though it seemed like such a long distance away, the path was one that my mom and I had walked every weekend when we visited my grandmother. Therefore, it seemed to me that it was "just around the block." The distance felt even shorter when I remember how loved my grandmother made me feel and how desperately I wanted to feel that way again.

The sounds of cows and horses echoed as I walked among pastures and dirt roads. Suddenly, out of a backdrop of blackness, a young man walked up to me. He asked me my name followed by many questions like "Where are you going, little girl?" and "What are you doing out this late at night?" and "Why are you lost?" I don't remember being afraid of him even though he was a stranger, but rather annoyed by him because he was distracting me from getting to my grandmother's house. Despite my assurance to him that I was NOT LOST, he would not let up as he walked along with me. "You should come home with me. I'll drop my stuff off and then I can walk you to her house," he said.

I said, "No. I know where she lives. I am NOT lost." Finally, after feeling tired of telling him that I was not lost, I agreed to let him walk me to my abuelita's house if that was what it would take to get there.

Since my mom was a single mom, my grandmother would help watch me. I had such a special relationship with her that I used to think she was my mom. My abuelita, Leonor, was left a widow when I was three. She continued to support her family by cleaning people's homes and washing laundry. The skill was all she knew, so she used it to support herself. I remember my abuelita ALWAYS telling me to study hard and get an education so that I wouldn't have it hard like her and my mom. Amidst her end-of-the-day exhaustion, I would sit on her lap, hug her and tell her: "Don't worry, abuelita. I'll go to school to get a good job and take care of you and you won't have to work any more." Each time I said it, I knew that it was what I was going to do.

My grade school years in Colombia seemed easy to me. I always did very well in school academically but not necessarily behaviorally. Even though I was a good student, I was not attentive. Whenever the teacher stopped talking, and we were left to study independently, there I was distracting others and getting into trouble. I do remember needing eyeglasses from a very young age, but I would not wear them all the time even though my prescription was very strong. My mom would say: "The doctor said you need to wear them to 'fix your eyes.'" I didn't know why my eyes needed "fixing" because I saw the same with and without my glasses. I didn't want to continue to be called *ojos de rana* or "frog eyes" by other kids in school if I did wear my glasses.

I attended school in Colombia until the fifth grade. My father, who I had met when I was 7, came to take me to live with him in the United States. It seemed like a dream—but not for the same reasons as many other immigrants. I was more enamored with the daddy that I had been missing as long as I could remember. Life in the United States proved to be very challenging—and far from the dream that I, or most immigrants, imagine. Almost immediately, I realized my dream was rooted in the realm of imagination. My first year here, my dad said he couldn't take care of me because of problems with his wife. He took me to live with his friend's family in Rockford and my dad visited me on the weekends.

I repeated fifth grade in my school in Rockford so I could focus on learning English and not fall behind. I already knew fifth grade work from Colombia. This was the first time I remember feeling challenged in school. I attended ESL classes in the morning and in the afternoon I would attend regular fifth grade classes entirely in English with the other fifth graders.

I became more withdrawn and timid. I loved fifth grade math class; I was the top student when it came to analytical coursework. But afternoon English class was another story. I sat there side-by-side with American students. The teacher called on different people to read aloud. To this day, I remember that sinking feeling and a voice within me that begged, "Please don't pick me." But she did call on me, and often, because I needed the most help. Stumbling over the words in my thick, Colombian accent, the kids would laugh at me. The words on the page were not only foreign but even seemed to blur in and out as I read aloud. I would go home, consumed by their scathing words and my boundless inadequacies. Over and over again, I practiced the vocabulary words after school on the way to the babysitter's house. The next day, however, the panic rose again and, worse, the truth: They didn't know Ingryd. They knew my accent. It defined me. Although I didn't realize it at the time, I started to lose me, Ingryd.

The following two years, my father took me back to live with him and his wife in Chicago. It was then when I found that my daddy wasn't the man who I thought he was. He was violent and an abuser by nature. As a result, my dream shattered into a thousand pieces. Other than school, I was always home alone. It was the first time in my life that I felt completely alone, but it was better than having my dad home with the constant anxiety and pounding of my heart, not knowing if any little noise was going to set him off.

By eighth grade, my mom had come to the live in Long Island and I went back to live with her. My English was significantly better and I completed school successfully with a scholarship to go to a very elite school. However, I KNEW I was different than the other kids. I started my first semester, my mom married and we moved to New Jersey with her husband and his children where I completed my first high school semester. This didn't seem to be the place for me either, and I started my second semester of high school in Kentucky, at the boarding school of Mount Saint Joseph Academy.

Although I was alone, the school was the first place I felt at peace. The Ursuline sisters became my family. Their focus was "the girls" and I was ONE of those girls. I felt loved and special for the first time since my abuelita. Although not wealthy like the other girls, they were also alone, so the playing field started to level. I would study ALL the time and I was in the top two in my class. Ingryd was coming back! I washed dishes in the convent to help pay for my tuition and finished my sophomore year there. I would love going to mail call right after school and get letters from my abuelita.

Unfortunately, the devastating news came one day that the Academy was closing and I had to finish high school somewhere else. That summer, my abuelita passed away too, unexpectedly. I didn't keep my promise of taking care of her. Guilt washed over me. I returned to Chicago with my dad and his wife where I knew what awaited me, but I had no choice. I graduated high school with a full scholarship to Mundelein College. My only memory: my dad didn't show up at the ceremony.

The few people who know this part of my story, always say: "Wow, you're such a strong person." I never really looked at myself that way, though. While I was going through it, I felt very alone like a burden being moved from place to place. I felt unloved and that I just wanted it to stop.

Just like that evening back in kindergarten, I took matters into my hands, responsibility for my life and replaced fear with determination …

The day after high school graduation, with five dollars in my pocket, I moved into an attic apartment of St. Genevieve's Parish in exchange for work as a weekend receptionist. My scholarship paid for my college and I worked part time at Sears Optical, where the next phase of my life started. If you think my teenage years were "bumpy", wait until I tell you about my rollercoaster college years and surviving optometry school despite my visual learning disabilities! That, however, will have to wait for my upcoming book, and I promise not to disappoint.

Now, you might be wondering if I ever made it to my abuelita's house that night. No, but even now, I see that I was never really alone. God has been watching over me and has always put angels in my path. When I followed the man to his home, he put me with his younger sister, and called the local radio station to tell them he had found a lost little girl. I remained safe until my mom picked me up.

So what made me a strong person? What has gotten me to where I am today and led me to fulfill half of my promise to my abuelita?

Reflecting back, I see that no matter how many changes, challenges or situations have come into my life, there has been consistency in having a heart felt-desired mission, fearless determination, and an unstoppable work ethic! My abuelita did what she had to so she could support her kids as a widow. My mom did what she had to do to be a single mom. And I just had to do what I had to do to keep moving forward and reach my goals.

So, whether you are rich or poor, those are qualities that we all possess. We just have to put them to USE … so when life happens, we don't let the sparks within us die. Rather, you should use the abilities you already have to achieve your mission.

# Dr. Ingryd Lorenzana

At the age of 10, Dr. Lorenzana emigrated from Bogota, Colombia to the United States. Although a high-achieving student, she struggled with reading, which led her to believe that it was due to English being her second language. Her determination to be the first in her family to graduate from college earned her a B.S. from Mundelein College but it was perseverance and vision therapy that got her a Doctorate from the Illinois College of Optometry.

The diagnosis and treatment of convergence insufficiency was pivotal to her success in optometry school and proved to be the cause for her lifelong reading struggles. It was then that, Dr. Lorenzana chose the specialty of Vision Learning Disabilities as the focus of her life work and went on to complete a Residency in Pediatrics – Binocular Vision and Perception at the Illinois Eye Institute.

In 2003, Dr. Lorenzana established Advanced Vision Center where she serves as Director for Pediatric and Adult Specialty Optometric Services.

In 2012, she founded the Vision and Sensory Integration Institute with the mission to improve the quality of life and to achieve maximum potential for those struggling with vision problems. Her exclusive groundbreaking neuroplasticity - sensory integrative treatment protocol incorporates the latest technology in the rewiring of visual neural pathways in treatment of Vision Learning Disabilities and/or rehabilitate visual function loss due to brain injury, trauma, concussion or stroke.

A highly sought after, international speaker, Dr. Lorenzana was named "3D Eye Doctor Of The Year" from Hollywood's 3D International and Advanced Media Society and the 2014 Influential Women in Business Award from the Daily Herald. However, she considers her greatest accolade to be the responsibility of making a difference in every patient's life.

Dr. Ingryd Lorenzana
Advanced Vision Center
19 E Schaumburg Road
Schaumburg, IL 60194
847-891-8003
drl@avconline.org
www.AVConline.org

# Starla Snead

## *The Serenity Prayer*
## *Many Lessons in Authenticity*

On a recent visit with my mother-in-law, I shared with her the possibility of participating in this project. She asked me what "overcoming mediocrity" meant to me. I couldn't really answer her at that time. That was the place I had to start.

Mediocrity, to me, means not living to my fullest potential; not using my God given gifts and abilities; not being authentic – that is, who I was created to be. It's not about where I live, what kind of car I drive, or who others think I should be. It's about my own self-esteem and living out my own potential. I am overcoming mediocrity.

"God grant me the serenity to accept the things I cannot change, courage to change the things I can and the wisdom to know the difference."

The Serenity Prayer is the common name for this prayer authored by the American theologian Reinhold Niebuhr (1893-1971). It has been adopted by Alcoholics Anonymous and other twelve step programs. A Serenity Prayer plaque hung on a wall in our house growing up in West Virginia. Little did I know how that would influence my life. My father was a recovering alcoholic. Despite his struggles with alcohol, he was a strong and faithful leader of our family. My father was a hard worker and a successful entrepreneur. I was twelve years old when he died at the age of 54 of a heart attack. The Serenity prayer on our wall helped teach me acceptance and a willingness to let go. The first step in reaching any goal or finding any understanding is to know that there will be things in my life that I cannot change. Once I accept the situation, that no matter how much I try, I will not be able to change it, I am ready to get on with what I can do to the best of my ability.

Growing up, I despised my name, Starla. It was different and unique. I was different and unique. I was a tomboy with a rebellious attitude from day one. Because I was different, I was made fun of. I never seemed to fit in no matter how hard I tried. I always wanted to go to college to study architectural design & drafting. After the death of my father, my dreams and goals were put on the sidelines. Survival was the major task at hand for the family, especially for my mom. My life progressed as a rebellious teenager leaving home as soon as I graduated high school at age 17. I began working at a local restaurant as a hostess/waitress. I set out to prove to the world that I was smart. I was somebody special and I could do it all on my own!

I began taking general education classes at the local community college. First year life was grand – working full-time, partying full-time and going to college full- time. I needed something stronger – Chemistry - -Women in Chemistry - - now that is where it's at.

Second year, when it came time for the core curriculum classes with more time needed for studying, I dropped out. I met my first husband shortly thereafter, who was also an alcoholic. The marriage lasted for 5 years. It took courage and wisdom to determine that this was not the right path for me. It was through this failed experience that I learned that God's guiding hand was with me every step of the way giving me courage and strength.

A customer came into the restaurant and told me about a program with the local college that was being sponsored by a large chemical company. All that was needed was to complete their program and they would hire you as a lab technician! With a continuing attitude of something to prove and $$ in my eyes, I completed my Associates degree in Chemical Technology and was hired as a lab technician in 1989. I thought that I had finally arrived. Little did I know that this was not God's plan for my life.

I developed chemical sensitivity to the chemicals that I was working with which required that I change positions within the company three different times due to severe allergic reactions. I finally ended up in the library. Even at this point in my life, I knew that I received my energy from people. Being around books and computers was suffocating. This is where I began regrouping again. I began learning about my skills, strengths and weaknesses through the Dale Carnegie Course offered by the company. I completed my Bachelor's degree in Human Resources Management in 1996 and began working to develop training courses for Chemists and Engineers for online database searching. This is where I met my current husband. We were married in 2000.

In 1998, another large chemical company bought out the company that I was working for. The plans were in the works to close the library so I left the company to become an environmental trainer. I traveled the state of West Virginia working with water operating systems providing training in chemistry, math and management. I loved the excitement of the job, but leaving on Monday, coming home on Friday and working weekends was not conducive to a happy marriage.

It was time to regroup again by asking the all too familiar question: "What do I want to do when I grow up"? I decided to quit my job and within 3 months miracle baby #1, Edward, was conceived. He was named after my father. He is my miracle baby because I was told in my teens that I was unable to have children due to severe endometriosis. This was something that I had struggled with for many years. My next career move was to be a stay at home mom – that's what all good moms do – right? My mom was a stay at home mom. My mother-in-law was a stay at home mom. I could not grasp the concept of dropping my kids off at daycare and I knew that I wanted to be there for them when they got home from school. Miracle baby #2, Erik, was born in 2005. This was a huge transition for me and continues to be because I also desperately wanted my career.

Calligraphy, the art of beautiful writing, always caught my eye along with painted flowers. I loved the beautiful handwriting and the flowing swirls. I had always enjoyed painting and doodling, but never would have considered myself creative. I saw an ad in our local paper for a watercolor flower class that was being sponsored by the West Virginia Calligraphers Guild. It was extremely inspiring! I joined the Guild in 2002 and became a class junky. I discovered that I was creative. My creativity was finally being unleashed in a constructive manner. My only goal was to write out the words to the Serenity Prayer. I was able to accomplish this goal and more by studying with some of the best calligraphers and artists in the world.

I began designing the bulletin covers for our church. The church was very gracious in allowing me to foster my creativity. I created the design by hand for the bulletin covers every Sunday for three years. I turned the bulletin covers into notecards at the request of my dear friend Julia. Thus began my initial business of notecards and commissioned work.

In 2009, my husband's job brought us to Bolingbrook, IL. This was another huge transition and growing curve. It's not easy to pick up and move from your family even if you are doing all the right things. Losing my creative support system was the hardest.

Since moving to Bolingbrook, IL I have been blessed to further my calligraphic studies with renowned calligraphers Timothy Botts and Reggie Ezelle.

I had bought a battery operated hand held engraver at a yard sale for fifty cents. I put it in my craft drawer. About a year later, my mom called and asked if I could put my fancy writing in glass. I had no clue, but I gave it a try. It was not only successful, but beautiful. Thus began Designs by Starla, Calligraphy and Engraving. Engraving has become a huge part of my business with engraving on wine bottles, glass and even wood. I was able to engrave the serenity prayer in wood which now hangs on my wall in our home – Serenity – peace beyond all understanding.

In 2013, I discovered Zentangle while searching for a new pattern to add to a calligraphy piece that I was working on and immediately fell in love with it. Zentangle is a way to create beautiful images by drawing structured patterns. In learning Zentangle, you start by creating patterns on tiles of paper that are approximately 4" x 4". After a few of those, I began Zentangling anything that had a blank surface. In November of 2013, I became a Certified Zentangle Instructor (CZT). Zentangle is now a part of the design aspect of my business as well as teaching.

In the process of making an ornament with Zentangle patterns on it, I really did not like how the pattern was going since there are no mistakes in Zentangle. I took an alcohol pad to remove the marker and the ink started spreading. The biggest light bulb ever went off in my head! I had alcohol inks stored in my craft drawer where my battery operated engraver had been. Decorating with alcohol inks is now the second design aspect of my business.

I find peace when I am being creative and using my gifts that God has bestowed upon me. I love experimenting and trying new ideas. Maybe chemistry is a part of my life after all. I am not afraid to fail but afraid that I might succeed. That would require authenticity - which is a continuous ongoing adventure. I am growing and maturing as my children grow and mature. They help to inspire me. I have come to like and embrace my name-Starla. It symbolizes my uniqueness. I cannot change my past but I can change how I live in the present. I pray daily for wisdom. My heart screams daily for being creative, unique, and different. The world and my own self esteem tell me that I don't fit in. Wisdom gives me the courage to follow my authentic voice.

The serenity prayer plaque that I have engraved hangs on our wall in our home. I wonder what influence this prayer will have on my children's lives....

# Starla Snead

Starla Snead holds an AS in Chemical Technology and a BA in Human Resources Management. Her study of calligraphy began in 2003 as a way for her to transition into her role as a stay-at-home mom. She became a professional engraver in 2011 and is now a Certified Zentangle Teacher (CZT). Starla loves working with kids and teaches Zentangle and other art classes at Summer Camps and through various scouting organizations.

Starla is the proud mother of two active boys 9 and 12. Both boys participate in scouting. Starla is Committee Chair/Advancement Chair for Cub Scout Pack 38 of Bolingbrook.

She is a member of First Baptist Church of Bolingbrook, where she teaches Sunday school, Vacation Bible School and sings with the Worship Team.

Starla is an active P.E.O. member which serves to support education in women.

Her professional organizations include:

- Chapter Leader for DPWN Plainfield/Naperville;
- Member of Chicago Calligraphy Collective
- Member of Washington Calligraphers Guild
- Member of Bolingbrook Chamber of Commerce
- Member of Plainfield Chamber of Commerce
- Member of Naperville Leads.
- Member of Chicago's Entrepreneurs Group

Starla Snead
Designs by Starla
620 Cochise Circle
Bolingbrook, IL 60440
630-754-7346
starla@designsbystarla.com
www.DesignsbyStarla.com

# Susan M. Sparks

## *The Riches in a Rag-Tag Resume*

My resume isn't one with a dazzling trajectory of upward mobility and success. For years, I considered this my greatest shortcoming.

Growing up within earshot of the feminist movement, every young professional woman emerged from college replete with a five and ten year plan, quantifiable goals, and an accelerator pushed to the floor.

I was no different. I landed an impressive, high-profile government job right out of college, only to be fired six months later. Stunned and shamed by my naiveté when it came to the real game of politics, I stumbled around working as an aerobics instructor, camera salesperson, substitute teacher, newspaper editor, on-air radio announcer, wedding photographer, bartender, life insurance claims processor, and temp worker typing up inventories of generic feminine hygiene products.

My rag-tag resume was a concern to me in those years I was supposed to be out taking the world by storm and rising to the top. I cringed every time someone asked me what I did. I couldn't say. I thought that I needed a great title, corner office, and big paycheck to prove my value. Instead, my vitae was a meandering menagerie of pursuits held together by a few generally-related skills.

Growing up, I wasn't on the college fast-track. I was a farm girl convinced that I would marry the boy down the road and be a farm wife. Rattled by the sudden death of my father when I was 16, I was faced with a new and frightening paradigm. I watched as my mother, then only 49 years at the time, became paralyzed by her new future – that of a widow, without a career other than the helpmeet she had been while raising a family along with corn, beans, cattle, hogs, and sheep. College was suddenly in my future, only to ensure that I could hold my own if the marriage idea didn't pan out.

In the midst of my meandering, I got married. We moved to his home town and he went into the family business. I took a position as the editor of the local paper. I was finally using my journalism degree. (That must mean I'm on my way.) But the family business thing didn't work out. He was commissioned as a naval officer that would take us on a journey that spanned the globe. For the next 20 years, my resume was whip-stitched together with the job de jour.

When you are married to a career naval officer, rank and promotion are the unfaltering framework. Success is defined only by one adjective: upward – raises, rank, and power. In contrast, I made do with whatever opening was available that I could tweak my skills enough to fill. Even my own spouse teased that I had a lousy liberal arts degree (read, low-paying).

With each move, I was thrust into a new world. Imagine, finding a place to live or waiting for base housing with only a couple suitcases of belongings, get the mail to catch up, set up bank account access, change car licenses, update insurance, secure new utilities, stock the fridge, unpack the boxes, and find a job. It's tricky enough just moving to a new town, but a foreign country doesn't allow much carryover from a stateside position, so I had to start over in a new venture while my husband's vacation days and seniority continued to accrue.

But this story isn't about feeling repressed or unappreciated. Instead, it is the awakening to the incredible life I've crafted from this random collection of previous positions.

With each new job application, I cringed when presenting the tapestry of odd jobs in my past. To add to the cringe-worthiness, I had to tell a potential employer that I would only be available for two, maybe three years at most. Despite my concerns, I managed to snag some pretty cool duties.

In Chicago, I schmoozed with famous speakers, such as Og Mandino, US Ambassador Jeane Kirkpatrick, and Brian Tracy while working at a speaker's bureau. In Sicily, I published freelance articles in various American magazines and raised two toddlers. In Washington, D.C., I frequented posh hotels and historic mansions, photographing weddings that cost as much as a modest home. Off to Guam and a host of new opportunities, working as a personal assistant for a Korean official's wife, then as an editor and writer for the navy base newspaper, covering super typhoons, earthquakes, and rescues at sea.

I frequently heard other military spouses complain when the commissary was out of milk (thanks to bandits in Southern Italy that held up the trucks) or about the shortage of videos at the rental place on base. While they whined that this was the worst place they had ever been stationed, I was walking the narrow streets of Sicily, savoring local cuisine and retracing historic steps from WWII campaigns. I was making the most of what I had – an up close look at pre-9/11 Europe.

From there, we returned to the states, settling into a bedroom neighborhood outside Washington, D.C. Culture shock set in, and during those times where my previous commissary choices had been yes or no, I was now overwhelmed by 17 types of orange juice or 34 varieties of sliced cheese. It was a true awakening to understanding what you need vs. what you want.

Washington D.C. was crowded, bustling, and expensive. Raising two preschoolers, I continued to write and worked as a wedding photographer. While I was able to stay home with my children during the week, their father was home on Saturdays, an ideal schedule for a wedding photographer.

But as the rhythm of military life dictated, within three years it was time to move again. This time across the Pacific to the tiny island of Guam. If you've ever had the fantasy of living the carefree life on a tropical island, I'm afraid I'll burst your bubble. There were biting, stinging things in the ocean, unexploded WWII ordnance scattered about in the jungles, unexplained power outages, mail took forever, TV shows were on a two-week delay (yes two-weeks) and you could drive the perimeter of the island in an afternoon.

Our time on Guam was rife with major events: SARS, Y2K and 9/11. Travel was stopped, our mail languished in Hawaii, and uncertainty was the order of the day. Add to that two super-typhoons within 10 days of each other and a couple hefty earthquakes. While my husband was temporarily stateside, my children and I hunkered in for 24 hours of wind and rain, only to be without electricity and water for two weeks in the aftermath of Super Typhoon Ponsongwa. We cooked Pop Tarts on a camp stove and slept on air mattresses in the carport, since the house was abloom in mold from the humidity and heat.

Our last move back to the states meant starting the job hunt all over again. In each interview, I hurried to point out the gaps and lapses in my work history – instead of concentrating on the fact that packing and moving a family of four for 10 moves in 20 years is the equivalent of a master's degree in logistics and organizational systems. That experience birthed my book, *The Student Life Jacket.*

After 20 years of roaming the globe, my marriage ended and shortly after, so did the first job that I hoped would be permanent. It was during this time that I picked up a copy of Jack Canfield's *Success Principles.* One entry in particular struck a chord – what is your version of success? I had only considered it was the version I had accepted fresh out of college; a fancy title and a big paycheck.

Yet, it wasn't a job title or a bank balance. My asset column was packed with the things I valued: creativity, passion, variety, freedom of expression, and fulfilling relationships. I realized I was a success, and this new chapter would be mine to write, both as an entrepreneur and an independent woman.

But I was also ticked off. In this new light, I realized that I had been robbed. I had robbed myself of confidence and contentment by constantly comparing my resume to those who worked their way up the ladder from assistant to executive.

In defining my own description of success, I realized that my perceived shortcoming was actually my greatest strength. I've lived multiple lives, each one supplying me with infinite experiences, environments, and memories. I have lived where other people only dreamed of visiting. I had explored different jobs and areas of interest all while being paid. I learned about new industries and people, and expanded my skill sets.

The stress I put on myself was that which I thought others expected of me. I was my harshest critic, letting other's attitudes about their careers influence my own. While others felt stuck in a field they had grown weary of, I had justification to change jobs faster than I could grow out a bad haircut. Today, my resume is a badge of honor, a multi-faceted platform that affirms my skills as an expert in adaptability. It reflects a colorful road of opportunities that allowed me to try possibilities while staying grounded in my original degree – that lousy, liberal arts photojournalism degree that has repeatedly slaked my thirst for adventure, serendipity, and variety.

Overcoming mediocrity does not mean that you have to be the richest person with the most impressive title in the room. It means embracing your own gifts and tapestry of experiences, taking pride in them, in the discovery of who you are, and how you inspire and bless others.

Each detour, odd job or temp position taught me to be a keen observer, pick up on nuances, and adapt to a new environment, all vital skills that I use in my work as a ghostwriter. I've worked in offices, military bases, and entrepreneur's basements, continually collecting nuggets of wisdom and experiences that reinforce my belief that comparison is a thief of our individuality and confidence.

Today, I am extremely blessed to work with interesting, inspiring men and women who look to me for help in spreading their message. Writing another's story helps us both. Those who fear writing find they can safely and confidently share their ideas and stories with the world. I can continue my eclectic collection of assignments that feeds my hunger for all things unique and unusual while building a close, collaborative bond with my clients. By the time we've finished, they HAVE written a book. Ours is an alliance that forces them to set an intention, identify their true purpose, refine their message, and promote themselves with a new awareness. I relish the diverse topics and clients I work with. Having such a varied backstory of my own, I am able to identify the unique components others have to offer. Much like sifting through the sands of someone else's story, I also discovered the riches buried in my own experiences.

We all have a story to share, yet we all have a bit of trepidation in revealing our backstory. Why would anyone listen? Who would care? The fact is, your story is a jumping off place for someone else. Before you doubt yourself and ask, what in the world do I have to offer? Make sure you are using the correct valuation. There are many measuring sticks in life, and a resume is only one of them. Knowing what you enjoy, what you love learning about, and practicing it is the richest reward.

# Susan M. Sparks

Susan M. Sparks is a writer, photographer, and author of *The Student Life Jacket*.

A story teller from an early age, Susan self-published her first book about wild horses in the 5th grade. She continued creating compelling content earning a B.S. degree in Photojournalism from Ball State University.

As the wife of a naval officer, she moved around the world to exotic locations, such as Sicily and Guam, and the not-so tropical Maryland and Illinois, observing, recording and reporting on the people and places. She adapted her talents to fit the location, working as a freelance writer, wedding photographer and Navy Public Affairs contractor punctuated by motherhood and a smattering of curious and quirky gigs in between.

Susan describes moving around the world, discovering new cultures, and keeping a family organized as an out-of-the-frying-pan-into-the-fire training program that included volcanic eruptions, earthquakes, and super typhoons along with the continual upheaval of several military moves.

Back home again in Indiana, Susan provides ghostwriting, editing services and encouragement to entrepreneurs, aspiring authors, and business owners through her company, ASAP Writing Services. Her book, *The Student Life Jacket,* is an organizer with a slice of motherly advice for college students and young adults.

Susan M. Sparks
ASAP Writing Services
209 Bayview Drive
Cicero, IN 46034
847-502-2494
Susan@ASAPWritingServices.com
www.ASAPWritingServices.com
www.SimplifiedbySusan.com

# Ursula Wachowiak
## *How The B.R.O.A.D. was Born and Reborn*

Back in the day, I didn't really think of my life as mediocre. I thought I did pretty well being both a mother and a professional. I experienced many of the typical ups and downs in life but nothing too earth-shattering. In my early 30's, I went to college to study psychology and I began to see life and the world with a whole new perspective. My studies opened my mind and my heart to the plights of others and my own. I quickly began to embrace a new me; a me that could do bigger things and be a bigger person.

When my son was 15 ½ years old, I made the difficult decision to become single and finish raising him on my own. I had never really been "on my own" and it was a scary endeavor. We struggled but we lived more than we ever had before. As a child, some of my family members rode motorcycles, my family put me on dirt bikes and quads, and I had always enjoyed the adrenaline. I taught my son in the 8th grade to ride a dirt bike, but it was during those early years of being single that I truly embraced the passion for motorcycling. My son and I took a motorcycle safety course together and the fuel had been poured on the fire.

Between renting motorcycles and trusted friends that would loan me bikes, I was riding regularly. My son got a bike of his own through a fluke and a caring friend (yes, I was jealous – but since he only had a permit I got to use it when he was in school). My outgoing personality, big mouth, and success as an event planner / organizer led me into a whole new world. I was organizing motorcycle rides, contacting friends to join, and researching events that we could attend as a group. Eventually my network became so large that I could not easily text or call the masses to organize things. Therefore, I created a group on social media called Ursula's Local Riding Buddies. It was a catch all place where we could share events and information related to motorcycling.

As the months turned to years, it seemed that there was never a shortage of friends or motorcycles to ride. However, I still didn't have my own bike. My son eventually turned into a man with his own life and flew the nest. At a car show in my then home town, a buddy told me that he had found a motorcycle that was perfect for me. I was as giddy as a school girl when I heard the details. The price did not break my small savings account completely, but it was one heck of a purchase for me. After the deal went down, I immediately rode over to my son's job to show off my first Harley Davidson. He could not believe that I had really done it – finally done it!! Naturally, I forced him to ride with me the following day.

Time continued to pass and except for the brutal winter days of Chicagoland you could almost always bet that my mode of transport was that 1995 Sportster. I enjoyed riding alongside my son and took motorcycle vacations with friends. I attended many more events because I had my own bike, and my riding group continued to grow in membership.

In March of 2012, life gave me a slap in the face – I lost my corporate job. That was a difficult economic time for our country and though I tried diligently I had no luck getting a job making anywhere near what would sustain my very simple life. I blew through the rest of my savings and the anemic 401k trying to keep my rent, utilities and insurance current. I had started a small side business in 1997 called The Write Hand. As the owner of The Write Hand, I provide virtual assistant support to entrepreneurs and small business owners. Anything that an assistant could do without being on-site, I could do for my clients. I had to push that venture a lot harder since I couldn't find a 'real job'. The harder I worked at it, the more I realized the potential and demand for my services. At some point during that process, a dream materialized…

I was still not making enough for basic living expenses. However, by my calculations if I didn't have to pay rent, utilities, and insurance on my car; I could live fine. But where could I live for free? With a bottle of wine given to me by a friend and a huge notebook, I began to form a plan. I was going to be homeless and live on my motorcycle. And so it began – The B.R.O.A.D. ™ journey (Babe Riding Out A Dream).

Once I shared my crazy idea with friends, the outpouring of support was overwhelming. People began to share information with me about other nomad motorcyclists which gave me ideas on how to successfully be homeless. Local biker related media and motorcycle groups began to share my story. In October of 2012, just seven months after losing my job, I was opening the doors of my apartment for an estate sale. My friends and strangers bought up nearly all of my possessions with the exception of a few things that I would leave in storage with my son. For my birthday later in October, my friends suggested a party / fundraiser to help increase the funding for The B.R.O.A.D. ™ journey. When it was said and done, I had $7,000 to my name.

I spent the winter living rent free between a generous friend and my son, while continuing to grow The Write Hand. I wanted to stick around for the holidays and for my granddaughter's first birthday in February 2013. Besides, trying to leave Illinois by motorcycle in the winter could be a deadly feat. I had told my friends and son that as soon as there was a break in the weather, I was going to make a run for it. I was first going to head south toward my parents and warmer weather. The weekend before my granddaughter's birthday, we held a party at one of our favorite hang-outs. It was a chance to see folks before I hit the road. My granddaughter's birthday and party were on Sunday, February 23, 2013. By then I was already living out of the bags I intended to carry on the journey and needed only to pack up my toiletries, sleeping bag, and laptop. Be it God or Mother Nature – somebody was watching over me because on Monday the weather in Chicagoland was 34 degrees and sunny. That was the day!! I bid a tearful farewell to my son, put my dog and belongings on the bike, and took off.

That first day was freezing cold and I had to stop often to care for my dog and ensure that we did not dehydrate or get hypothermia. I made it into central Indiana after dark fell and the temperatures dropped. I got a cheap hotel and rested. Day two was actually worse as the rain added to the bitter cold. But day three warmed up and I finally made it to my Dad's house in Georgia. I promptly fell sick and hung out for nearly two weeks visiting my family before truly starting the journey. My dog would retire her motorcycle days and stay with my Dad.

I left Georgia the first week of March and headed into Florida at my leisure. From that point on, my days consisted of working as my schedule dictated from free Wi-Fi spots when available or my own Wi-Fi Hotspot. My business allows me to work when my clients need me so the hours are never exactly set. If I was not working, I was riding and stopping to see the scenery in the USA. Where did I sleep? I had learned from another nomad and experimented on my own with sleeping in what I call God's country. I found spots in the wilderness and abandoned buildings that provided hidden protection and an area for my tent and motorcycle. The details of how to accomplish this are rather lengthy but it was important to be legal and cautious.

I traveled like this every day. Unless I was camping on-site at a particular event, I never stayed in one place more than a night. As word spread, some of my friends would put me in contact with their own friends and family in areas where I was or was going to. This gave me the opportunity not only to meet even more amazing people but also to enjoy a few couches and beds –my back was ever so grateful.

For six months I traveled and toured. It was **THE MOST PEACE** that I had ever experienced in my life. The daily challenge of where would I sleep no longer seemed like a scary chore but became part of the awesomeness of the adventure. On July 17, 2013, my dream abruptly ended. Two miles across the Minnesota border from Wisconsin, a young man trying to pass a semi-truck in a deep curve hit me head-on. Emergency responders did all they could for me but as the helicopter landed on the hospital rooftop, the last things that I saw in that life were blue skies and sunshine – I had died.

Four days later, I emerged from a coma and saw the most beautiful face on the earth – my son. I knew that I had been in an accident but I was not fully aware when I woke. My medical team welcomed me back and very promptly set to the task of explaining my ordeal. I was given the option of enduring many surgeries that would likely not produce best-case results, or I could have my left leg amputated below the knee. The doctor left me with my son to discuss it. It took no more than two minutes and my son already knew the answer, the leg had to go. The sooner the leg was gone, the sooner I could heal and let technology get me back on my feet.

A whole new adventure began. It was not one that I was prepared for nor was it much fun. I spent eight months living with my Dad in Georgia while recovering and eventually got a prosthetic leg. During that recovery, one of the things that helped me get through all the depression and confusion was a series of videos I produced on YouTube called, "Doing It with The B.R.O.A.D. ™" These videos served as insight for my family, friends, and followers on social media and were based on my daily life and how I managed my disability. The series was very popular and the feedback gave me exceptional strength to continue keeping my head held as high as possible given the circumstances.

As my recovery progressed, it was clear that I could not live with my Dad forever. It was time to make some changes. My son came to visit and for a week he, my Dad, and I converted an enclosed 7' x 12' v-nose trailer that I could live in and pull with a used pickup truck. I intended to hit the road again. At a few points during my recovery, I was blessed to have a few folks that put me on the back of a motorcycle to see how my mind and soul would react. I did well and missed the ride. A leg amputee from social media saw that I was near him during a visit I had with my Mom in South Carolina. He offered me lunch with him and his wife which I gladly accepted. At this point, I already had my second prosthetic and was able to bear full weight and not use crutches. However, I was still learning how to walk. After lunch, he invited me back to his house. While there, he brought out his motorcycle and coaxed me to sit on it. He is a persuasive man that had already lived what I was going through. After a while, he waved me off to drive the bike down the road. I was nervous as all hell, but I did it. One mile down and one mile back – that was all I needed.

On Easter Sunday in 2014, just eight months after my crash, I hooked up the trailer to the truck and bid farewell to Georgia. A new adventure and new life were on the horizon. I again made great efforts to rebuild The Write Hand and traveled the USA with visions of going west, where I had not yet gone. This time I had to use campgrounds. Although I chose the least expensive sites with the fewest amenities, it was still running me about $25 a night. Biker events and meeting new folks and old friends along the way were just a few of the perks of this new adventure. In June of 2014, I made it back to Illinois and settled in for a six week visit with my family and friends. It was during this visit that a girlfriend loaned me her extra motorcycle. I rode once again with my son. It was a delight that I thought might never be possible again. I rode with friends and they helped me begin the search for a motorcycle that would suit my new condition. So it was that on July 15, 2014, two days short of the year anniversary of my crash, I purchased a 2004 Harley Davidson Heritage Softail. I loaded the motorcycle in the trailer and made my way back to where it all crashed and burned in Minnesota. My friends and I had a motorcycle run through my crash site and I was able to spend some time with the young man that hit me. He and I affixed the keys to my long gone old Sportster on the tree where the crash occurred.

The 2nd Leg of The B.R.O.A.D. ™ journey continued for a full eight months until it finally wore on me so much physically and financially that I had to be smart and settle down – at least for a little while. I chose an area in Western North Carolina with some of the most amazing roads for motorcyclists. I entertain visiting guests and share my piece of heaven with them, whether they are on two wheels or four. I have started a giving project called The SOX

Program where we collect odd socks in good condition which are donated to amputees in places like veterans' homes or children's hospitals. I have created another YouTube series called, "Amp'd Rider Project" which showcases the stories of amputees that ride motorcycles, the professionals that modify motorcycles for amputees and healthcare providers that have to remove limbs for a living and build prosthetics for our quality of life.

It is easy to see that my life has not been mediocre since I found my passion for motorcycles and I intend never to be mediocre again. When I talk about my triumph over this disaster, I always tell people, "If I had the choice of keeping my leg and never doing the original journey, I would not change a thing and would gladly give up the leg again." The human mind and spirit are the most amazing wonders that should be built up and cherished. Let no other human ever dictate what your life can become.

# Ursula Wachowiak

Ursula Wachowiak grew up simply like many of us. She became a wife, mother, and professional. It would seem that she enjoyed a great deal of success along with some of life's typical challenges. It was during the hardest of times that she made a choice to not only be her own boss but to do so while becoming homeless. Using her years of professional expertise, she built The Write Hand, LLC; a Virtual Assistant business. She sold nearly everything she owned to travel the United States on her Harley Davidson. She worked hard, slept in the woods and abandoned buildings, toured the country, and wherever she went, she gave inspiration to everyone that she encountered.

A tragic accident that occurred as Ursula toured the country resulted in the loss of part of her left leg. This B.R.O.A.D. ™ yet again rose to her greatest during the hardest of times. She rebuilt The Write Hand, LLC, bought another Harley Davidson, and toured the country again. She now has a much larger following that spans more than just the motorcycle community. She says, "You can hit me, You can break me, You can make me bleed, but as long as I'm still breathing; the road is where I'll be."

Ursula Wachowiak
The Write Hand, LLC
the_write_hand@yahoo.com
www.imurwritehand.wordpress.com

# Dori J. Mages

## *12 Attributes Strong Women Need for Success*

Have you ever wondered how some women seem to be successful at everything they try? Have you noticed that these strong, successful women never seem to stop achieving and doing? Have you ever found yourself asking, "What do they have that I don't?" Or, "How can I use what I have to be like them?" If you have, you're not alone. Asking these questions proves that you are well on your way to being a strong woman.

How do you do it all? I'm asked this question on a regular basis. I am a wife, mother of three, business owner, licensed clinical social worker, and public speaker. Since I was a teen, my mother would ask me facetiously, "Dori, you know that there are only 24 hours in a day, right?" My immediate response has always been, "No, I'm pretty sure that my day has more."

While many people feel overwhelmed when they have a lot to do, I thrive on multi-tasking and NEVER settle for mediocrity. Over the years, I have met many strong women with a similar take on life and have found that they seem to share twelve common attributes that impact how they live their lives, work in their desired fields, and raise their families.

**1. Strong women don't wait for something to happen, they make it happen:**

I'm not a super woman. I simply have a lot on my agenda every day and I strive to accomplish it all. I always have. I recently purchased a one-of-a-kind art canvas that inspires me. It says, "If you don't go after what you want, you'll never have it. If you do not ask, the answer will always be no. If you do not step forward, you will always be in the same place."- paraphrasing Nora Roberts. I don't easily take no for an answer and if I want something, I don't wait for it to happen, I make it happen. This is the cornerstone of self-advocacy, an important skill I teach my own kids as well as the kids we work with at North Shore Family Services.

**2. Strong women do the best they can with what they have:**

I grew up on the North Shore, in a prestigious suburb of Chicago, but lived in a very modest three bedroom split level home. My father worked long hours as a pharmacist and came home late into the evening to a warm, home-cooked meal. My mother was a strong woman, a stay-at-home mom, who ensured that my sister and I had everything our friends had: piano and ice skating lessons, camp, and religious school. I even had ONE pair of the $50 jeans that all the kids wore in the '80s.

My mother cooked every night except Saturday night- date night. My parents never went anywhere fancy, but they made time for themselves. They did the best they could with what they had.

As a parent and professional working with children and teens, I stress to parents that the quality of time spent with their kids is more important than the quantity of time spent with them. For financial reasons, it is often necessary for both parents to work, which leaves less quantity of time, but that doesn't have to negatively impact the quality.

**3. Strong women give their best effort to every endeavor:**

In high school, I was a hard-working student who earned 'A's and 'B's and enjoyed contributing to class discussions. I never saw a 'C' on my report card until my senior year when I took Calculus with peers who later attended Ivy League schools.

Until that time, I never felt like the dumb kid in class. I was determined to succeed. I gave my best efforts by studying every day and seeking help from the instructor when needed. However, I knew I was not going to be an 'A' student in Calculus.

Through this experience, I developed empathy for the kids who struggled with learning disabilities, behavioral and attentional problems, and other adversities. These were the kids who, no matter how hard they tried, were not performing as well as they would have liked. Personally, I was determined not to allow a poor grade define me or my success.

Today, I don't expect straight 'A's from my own children or from the kids and teens in our practice, but I do expect them to give their best effort. At North Shore Family Services, we tell all of the kids and teens that any setback or disability they have may be a **reason** for their struggle, but it doesn't justify using it as an **excuse** not to succeed.

## 4. Strong women know the importance of quality friends:

I wasn't even close to being the most popular girl in school, but I had a few great friends from every part of my life. I still keep in touch with many of these friends today both in real life and via social media. I strongly believe that having a few great friends is far more important than many casual friends. I share this lesson with all the children in my life with the hope that it teaches them the value of friendship.

In high school, I had **theater** friends I met through my love of performing in music, theater, and dance productions at New Trier High School and in my community. I had **work** friends at my first job where I worked in the box office of a local movie theater. I also had very close friends in my **youth group,** where, as a senior, I was a board member of my local chapter and traveled for local and international conventions, sharing inspiration with other teenagers and leaders in our community.

Although popularity and acceptance seem vital for middle school and high school kids, I believe that strong women know that success is not measured by the number of friends you have, but by the number of friends who have your back.

## 5. Strong women never settle for good enough:

I was in the top 18% of my high school class of more than 750 kids, but I worried that I wouldn't be accepted into the University of Illinois at Urbana-Champaign's coveted Liberal Arts program.

Unlike many of my peers at New Trier, I had reason to worry: without in-state tuition, my parents couldn't afford to send me to the out of state Big 10 schools where I was also accepted. As an independent and introspective young woman, I believed that the smaller in-state schools would not sufficiently challenge and interest me both socially and academically. I wanted to attend a large school where I could experience everything it had to offer.

Although I worried about many things, the pressure always came from within me. It didn't come from my parents. They would tell me, "A 'B' is good enough" and I would reply, "But I want an 'A'!" I never settled for good enough.

Today, I challenge kids and teens to compete with themselves, not with those around them.

## 6. Strong women use their fears or anxiety to propel them, not stop them from achieving:

My college roommate, Sara, called her dad crying every time she had a test during our freshman year. She'd say, "Daddy, I don't know anything! I'm going to fail!" When her father gently reassured her that she could do it, Sara immediately got off the phone and was ON A MISSION! She made notecards. She made notecards of her notecards. She then quizzed all the students in our dorm on all the information until WE were the ones who became anxious when we realized we didn't know what she knew.

Today, we tell the kids and teens in our practice that when they become anxious, they need to utilize that tension to propel them forward and to push them harder toward success.

## 7. Strong women can decide what they need to succeed:

I have always been a very social person. As a young child, I made new friends everywhere. Now, my own children complain that I talk to everyone: at the grocery store, in restaurants, anywhere.

In college, I was excited to meet new people, so I joined a sorority. I loved social events: parties, football games, and dances. What I didn't love was a group of other college students telling me when I had to study, who my date would be for a dance, what I would wear, where I would live, etc. It wasn't until three weeks before the end of my freshman year that I realized that I could still be social on my own terms. To paraphrase Glinda in "The Wizard of Oz," I "always had the power."

Those who know me now are not surprised that I left sorority life. They're also not in the least bit shocked that I didn't love participating in playgroups when my children were little. I founded my own private social work practice because when you know how to do something and do it well, you can make your own decisions about how to achieve it.

## 8. Strong women make a path for success:

When I began college, I had already earned college credit from Calculus and Spanish courses that I took in high school. I knew I could graduate a semester early if I kept a rigorous college course load. At a young age, I wanted to pursue a profession where I would help children and families. I thought that becoming a divorce attorney was the answer. I jumped into my path and joined the Pre-Law Club where I soon became a board member. Because I was successful in math, I also envisioned pursuing an MBA in five years before attending law school.

## 9. Strong women know when to veer off the planned course:

My career path plan changed with a few pivotal events during my college years. During the summer prior to my sophomore year, I worked for an attorney in an office with several other self-employed attorneys. I answered the phones, typed documents, and performed general office duties. I couldn't wait to learn about day-to-day life as an attorney!

On my first day, I met HIM, the ONE. He was a twenty-six year-old lawyer who had started a law practice with a partner just four months earlier. They shared a 10'x10' office they rented from my summer boss. Gary was intelligent, funny, and charming and I really enjoyed spending my work days with him. He was tall, dark, and handsome too. We joked, laughed, and worked hard. We became good friends that summer and six weeks before I was to return to college, he finally mustered the courage to ask me out on a date. He was (and is) a collection and real estate attorney and I could NOT, for the life of me, understand how he liked his job. I would ask him, "People pay you to get the money owed to them in the first place? And, they're happy with that?" I also asked, "So, you argue with people all day?" I realized then that my career path choices were in need of a shift.

When I returned to college that fall, I took my first (and last) accounting class. It was then that I questioned whether an MBA was in the cards for me. In accounting, I felt like an idiot. I didn't understand the concepts and I was completely in over my head. I dropped the class and was torn between being disappointed in myself for quitting something because I was unsuccessful and cheering for myself because, for the second time in my life, I knew when to stop doing something that I knew in my heart and mind wasn't a good fit for me.

When I dropped my accounting class, I added an Abnormal Psychology class. I was in love! I began learning that people's experiences and the way they think about them directly impact their actions.

**10. Strong women find smart people to help them:**

I began to wonder what I could do with a degree in psychology, so I met with an advisor in the psychology department. She had a master's degree in social work (MSW) and told me about the differences between pursuing careers in psychology and social work. I weighed my options and decided to pursue a graduate degree in social work.

Later in my career, when I opened my own practice, I hired a bookkeeper, a biller, and an accountant. I found smart people to help me, so I could concentrate on helping the children, teens, and families doing what I love to do and what I do best: therapy.

**11. Strong women gain experience to make them stronger:**

I graduated a semester early from college, got married seven months later, and began attending graduate school three weeks after getting married. I attended graduate school part-time so I could continue to work and gain real-life experiences while pursuing my degree.

While in graduate school, I worked in a foster home with teenage boys. I was only a few years older than some of the oldest kids, but I connected with them and absolutely loved my job. After graduate school, I worked as a school social worker for seven years before subsequently joining two private practices. At various hospitals, I worked in day treatment programs and in-patient psychiatric programs. More recently, I conducted psychiatric assessments in emergency departments to determine the need for hospitalization or other services for clients in crisis. I also collaborated with other child therapists from many disciplines at a clinic prior to founding my own practice in 2012.

When I opened my practice, I had been married for 18 years and had three children. My strategies with children and teens did not come from information I learned in a book, but from real-life experiences with former clients and my own children. I don't pretend to know all the answers or to be a perfect parent. Instead, I utilize my experiences to give the kids, teens, and parents tools that will be most helpful to them.

**12. Strong women aren't afraid to be themselves and do the right thing:**

Two of my favorite quotes have become my mantras. The first is: "Be who you are and say what you feel because those who mind don't matter and those who matter don't mind."- Dr. Seuss. With teenagers, I add the part about using tact. Teens will often try to justify being mean and insist they are "just telling the truth" when it is hurtful to others.

I don't pretend to be someone I am not. And, whenever my own kids question why they have to do something difficult or unpleasant, they know I will tell them my second mantra: "Do the right thing because it's the right thing to do." I always tell them that they will sleep soundly at night knowing they did the right thing, even if it was not their preferred choice.

Recently, my husband's cousin Cori, a marital and family therapist in California, questioned my philosophy about doing the right thing. She asked how I could know what would be the right thing to do and decided that someone must have influenced me at a young age. She asked if I am often disappointed because most people DON'T KNOW what that is.

It was my mother who influenced my beliefs on doing the right thing. I told Cori that I don't necessarily get disappointed, but I am often surprised by others' lack of knowledge and awareness of "proper" social protocol. When their actions don't align with what I believe is the right thing to do, I don't get offended or disappointed. I can be content in knowing that their "misbehavior" is not a reflection of how they feel about me. It's not malicious. It's simply a lack of knowledge.

The knowledge of right and wrong is vital, so I model that with my own children and the children and teens at work. I want them to be proud of their strengths and be aware of how their own actions affect others. Disappointment in others only takes away from their own strengths and successes.

Hmmmm. Perhaps there is a thirteenth attribute of strong women: we are not easily disappointed.

## Dori J. Mages

Dori J. Mages, MSW, LCSW is a licensed clinical social worker who has worked with children, teens, and families since 1994. In 2012, she founded her growing therapy practice, North Shore Family Services, LLC, offering services at two locations in the Chicagoland area. With the motto "Encouraging Children, Engaging Teens, Empowering Families," she and her colleagues guide clients to develop and maintain relationships, adjust to family changes, manage and re-purpose undesirable behaviors, and improve problem-solving skills.

As a wife and mother of three, Dori knows first-hand the joys, struggles, and effective strategies needed to help kids and teens grow into self-reliant, responsible adults. She is a highly acclaimed speaker on issues related to children, teens, parenting, and families. Dori also offers powerful presentations on effective communication skills necessary for personal and professional success. She has appeared on ABC and NBC news and has presented to a wide range of parent, school, professional, and clinical organizations.

Dori J. Mages, MSW, LCSW
North Shore Family Services, LLC
420 Lake Cook Road, Suite 121
Deerfield, IL 60015
2528 N. Lincoln Ave, Suite 116
Chicago, IL 60614
847-668-4295
info@northshorefamilyservices.com
www.NorthShoreFamilyServices.com

# Dede Schwartz
## *Determined To Achieve*

It was a big day in the third grade in 1959. We were getting ink cartridge pens and could choose either red, green or blue ink. Miss Lewis, the teacher, called each student up to the front of the classroom and handed them their choice of pen, smiling and congratulating them. I excitedly waited for my name to be called. I already knew that I was going to pick the red cartridge. My name wasn't called, so I raised my hand, asking if she forgot me. Miss Lewis responded in front of the whole class, "You don't get a pen, you didn't pass the penmanship test. I felt my face go hot, my heart began beating loudly in my chest and I began to cry. I felt ashamed, several students laughed and I heard someone say that I was dumb.

I didn't tell my parents what happened when I got home that day. I thought they would be mad at me. I acted like everything was okay and went out to play with my friends. That became a pattern for me. I buried the sad emotions and masked my shame by being fun to be with and happy all the time.

School remained a struggle for me, often getting poor grades. My parents were told every year that I was an under achiever. They would tell me to study harder. I hadn't been taught to study and didn't know how. I was often feeling lost and confused in school. It didn't appear that any of my friends had the same problems with school that I had. I didn't talk about the struggle because my shame ran so deep.

College was expected in my family. My older brother was already in college and doing well. I had a low grade point average and test scores. My parents would discuss this dilemma but not include me in any of the discussions. It was decided that if the school my older brother went to would accept me, that's where I would be going. I was accepted to Bradley University, with the stipulation from the university that I go to summer school prior to the fall semester. I barely passed the classes but was now on my way to college.

It was now 1969. The world was changing. There was Woodstock, hippies, free love, Vietnam, war, death and pain. I had no idea what I wanted to major in. The accepted choices were to be a teacher or a nurse. I didn't want to be either. My parents told me I was going to major in education, be a teacher and that was it. There was an unspoken rule in my home that my brothers and I didn't have a voice or choice in any major decisions with regard to our lives. This caused more frustration and continued to reinforce the shame I felt because whatever I said, especially if it was negative or contrary to what they felt or believed, I would be discounted. Something inside of me festered and because I didn't discuss my emotions or feelings, I snuffed them out by doing drugs and having good times away at school.

I was a dreamer. I loved music, dancing, singing and having fun. I wasn't ready to settle down. I also knew at that time feeling I was too dumb to do anything that would elevate me to where I felt everyone else was. I was still hearing the students laughing at me in my head. I didn't fight for myself and was miserable inside. I still hadn't spoken these feelings out loud. I felt wooden and fake. I was afraid to take risks and I wasn't encouraged to take them. Playing it safe, doing it their way ensured me a happy life, so they said....

I failed out of Bradley University after my sophomore year. I was ashamed as were my parents. I let them down. I transferred to Columbia College, a fine arts college in Chicago. The school was willing to take me. It was a fine arts college, where professionals in their field taught the classes. I majored in creative writing and literature. However, upon graduation, without a teaching degree there was little I could do with it.

I was groomed in my family to get married, work a few years and then have a family and be a stay at home mom. The prerequisite was going to college where I would meet the "man of my dreams" thus being able to live happily ever after. I married at 21 while still in college. I was feeling the pressure because many of my friends and family members were getting married at that time. It felt like I was playing house and I truly didn't understand the meaning of what it was to be married. We didn't love each other, **"How could I love someone when I didn't love myself?"** We had two children and were divorced after 9 years. It was 1982 and I was now a single mother of a 2 and 5 year old. I was 30 years old. I lived in the same community that I grew up in. I was the big topic of gossip due to the divorce. It brought shame to my parents again and I dove deeper into feelings of self-doubt and again masked it by acting happy.

I lived in a community of married families, so I took the easy way out and got married again one year after my divorce. I was playing house again, only this time my husband had been widowed and had a 3 year old son. We were the "Schwartz Bunch", blending yours, mine and eventually our own child. I felt safe again and saw how pleased and relieved my parents were that I had someone who would take care and provide for me and my children.

Several years into the marriage, I was beginning to feel trapped. I began to feel resentment at being dependent on someone to support me financially. I didn't have many skills to speak of to get a good job. Therefore, I took the easy way out again and stayed frustrated and unhappy with myself. We made a big decision to move away from the town that I grew up in. I was excited to have a fresh start. I could find something that I felt was missing, buried so deep inside of me. We moved to Naperville, Illinois in 1988. It wasn't as easy to make friends at 37 and I was often lonely. I played a lot of tennis and volunteered at my children's schools.

I began reading books on self-esteem and following your intuition. Something was calling me to give school another try. I researched the options at the College of DuPage, looking at what associate degrees or certificates were available. It had to be an easy path because I was so scared to fail again. I took career counseling. I was told I would be good in social services, sales and education. So then social services resonated with me.

Two of my childhood friends came to visit and we were preparing to go to our 20th high school reunion. They asked me what I was planning on doing, **"with the rest of my life".**

They both worked full time in professional jobs. One of them had children and the other did not. I told them defensively that my full time job was raising my 4 children!! The dummy complex was racing through my brain. I had never talked about it. A voice inside said to me, **"tell them!!"**

I remember taking a deep breath and softly spoke my truth out loud. I told them I had an interest in going to the College of DuPage and entering the Human Services program for a certificate in Addictions. They were happy and excited for me. I began to making excuses as to why I wasn't doing anything about it. One friend told me I was good with people, kind and empathic. She felt this was a good beginning for me **"Me going back to school? Really? I'm so dumb, I don't know how to study. What if I fail? Would I be a good counselor?"** Something that day finally took the laughing students in my third grade class out of my head and I began to hear my girlfriends from middle school, urging me and encouraging me on.

I entered my first class, and was more excited than I ever thought possible. I was 40 years old and back in school. I enjoyed what I was learning and it didn't seem so hard this time. I was beginning to breathe a little easier inside. **"There may be a place for me somewhere after all."** I had taken 15 credit hours and was on my way when tragedy came to my family, changing all of our lives forever.

My older brother, Richard, age 43, was shot and killed while out of the country. **"OH MY LORD, MY BROTHER IS DEAD!!"** Remember all of those sad and negative emotions I had buried since third grade? Now was the time to feel them and I didn't know how. I had loved my brother so much. We were close and if I shared something about myself, it was always to him. He never judged me. My grief was consuming as it also was for my parents and younger brother, Brad. It was so difficult to talk about it and I didn't know anybody who had experienced the loss of a sibling. I was depressed and closed. I stopped going to school. I walked around angry all the time, crying on the inside and not knowing how to deal with the grief, the devastating grief.

I was ill every month the first year after his death. My doctor was checking a bad cough and infection that I had and noticed a mole on my back and told me to have it looked at. It turned out to be melanoma skin cancer. I was 40 years old, my brother was dead, my parents struggling with painful grief and now I had cancer. My oncologist at our first meeting asked me what kind of year I had. I began to sob, telling him that my brother had been killed. It was the first time that I was able to release some of my pain. He explained that the suppression of emotions can cause huge stress on the body as it had for me.

A light bulb went off in my head. **"Stress can cause cancer."** I tucked that inside my brain. I resumed school and after another year and ½, I had my certificate to become an Addictions counselor. I found a job that I enjoyed at Linden Oaks Hospital in Naperville, Illinois. I was able to be a working woman, mother and wife. However, my depression was getting worse. I was afraid to go to therapy. I would sob in the parking lot before entering work, put on the mask I was so good at doing, then spend the day helping people deal with their lives.

I felt that I didn't matter enough to get help and I was still in a state of denial. I finally made the call and found a wonderful therapist at the urging of my cousin, who knew and understood me well.

I went to therapy weekly and slowly with the help of her kindness and empathy, I began feeling safe enough to open up about the grief of my brother, my cancer, feeling dumb and having low self-esteem. I was 46. I went to counseling for 4 months and when I was finished, I felt stronger.

I was able to laugh again, to see the joy of my children and engage in their lives fully again. I came to understand that by not opening up about my feelings, I wasn't able to feel validated. I was beginning to learn that I mattered.

I continued working as an addictions counselor, but didn't feel challenged. I had a bachelor's degree and would need a master's degree in order to make a higher salary, and move to the Psych Department for mental health. In 1998, at age 48, I received a call from a recruiter at National Louis University, asking if I would be interested in coming to hear about a program in the psychology department in Health Psychology. She explained what it was. My brain went back to my oncologist saying stress can cause cancer. I was beginning to link the stressors of peoples' lives to illnesses. I said yes without hesitation. It was the first time I made a decision that felt right and I didn't feel the need to discuss it with anyone. Three months later, I was in graduate school in Health Psychology going for my masters with the goal of getting my LCPC one day and moving to the Psych department at Linden Oaks Hospital. I wanted to be a group therapist.

I became mastered in Health Psychology. I loved what I was learning, becoming passionate about taking care of ourselves. I became an Adjunct Professor in the Psychology department and I was working in the job that I loved, as a clinical therapist in the Adult Outpatient Psych program at Linden Oaks Hospital. I helped the patients learn how to feel the emotions as I had learned to do. I was able to help them identify the causes of stress, grief and loss and support them as they struggled to regain their health and wellness.

I was going for my yearly mammogram at age 57, when I was diagnosed with breast cancer. It was 2009. I went through radiation after having a lumpectomy. I worked throughout my radiation and learned a lot about my strength and determination. It was a very difficult time. However, I was determined to get through it with a positive attitude, trusting the process. I wanted to live, be healthy and happy.

My marriage, had been struggling for some time, and during my cancer, there wasn't much support. I wanted to leave the marriage and was beginning to feel that I had the choice. I was making a decent living and could support myself on my own. The feeling of dependency was no longer an issue. I began to look at what wasn't working in the marriage and my life. I was willing to be aware of the faults within the marriage by both of us and then willing to make a choice. I chose to feel my feelings, knowing that as a survivor, not just of cancer, but of life that I would be okay.

I left my husband in 2011 at the age of 59. I did the Avon Breast Walk that same year, raising $1800.00. I meditated and continued a deeper and loving interest in spirituality and God. I felt happy, proud and finally no longer dependent on anyone but myself. I forgave myself for holding on to negative emotions that I carried about myself and not allowing my voice to be heard. I lovingly forgave my parents as I came to realize they did the best that they knew how. I realized how much they loved me and let it rain over me as I have learned to love myself

I recently left Linden Oaks Hospital after 10 years as a clinical therapist and I have learned my craft well. I have worked with all populations and all mental illnesses and life transitions. I am in private practice at True North Clinical Associates in Wheaton, Illinois. I specialize in mood disorders, grief/loss issues, health related issues and life transitions such as death, divorce, adjustment disorders, self-esteem. I give speeches on mindfulness and motivation.

I have gratitude for all of my life's lessons. I love that little girl who didn't pass her penmanship test in third grade taking her everywhere I go. She has grown into a happy and confident woman still determined to live the best life she can with love, joy and gratitude.

I teach my patients and clients the positive affirmations that I have learned and choose to use myself on a daily basis. I want to share them with you, the readers, too. Blessings to you all.

1. **I Matter** – learning to understand we all matter in this world.

2. **Gratitude** – giving thanks for all of our blessings in our lives, focusing on the positives.

3. **Trust the Process** – being mindful of trusting that life will work as it is meant to.

4. **It Is What It Is** – reality check that it is our thoughts that change what is really happening, not our emotions.

5. **Forgive Yourself** – understanding it is okay to let go of hurt and pain to ourselves or others.

6. **I Have A Choice** – the choice to say yes or no depending on what we want, not what others want.

7. **Speak Your Truth** – when we speak our truth of what is inside of us, we are heard.

## Dede Schwartz

Dede is full of energy and enthusiasm. She encourages a warm and welcoming approach to counseling where clients begin to relax and let their protective barriers down to freely express themselves. Dede uses a direct and honest approach with a variety of treatment modalities. She is passionate about empowering her clients and helping them achieve well-being and hope. Dede comes to True North following a long career working with patients at Linden Oaks Hospital, in Naperville, Illinois, both in the inpatient and day treatment programs. Dede taught in the Undergraduate Psychology program at National Louis University and lectures throughout the Chicago area on topics related to both physical and mental health.

True North Clinical Associates
55 E. Loop Road, Suite 203
Wheaton, IL 60189
www.TrueNorthClinical.com
630-653-1000 Office
630-653-1010 Fax

Dede Schwartz, LCPC
630-292-6365
dede1251@aol.com

# Debra Sunderland
## *It is All in What You Tell Yourself*

I love that not only do we all have a story, but we are also a story unfolding each moment. My strength and passion for daily growth stems from the beauty and freedom of mindful choice, and I encourage others to seek the same as well. The unfortunate reality is that life can be very painful and unexpected. As soon as I realized that I can't fight life, but I can fight my mind and my choices, I broke open to joy, peace, and direction.

My journey is one of living in extreme pain and fear under a physically and emotionally abusive mother and an alcoholic father. The unbearable torture that I endured made it to the news, neighbors, school and police many times. However, I was still left to survive within my family. I had no one to rescue me, except for myself. My way to survive in early life, was to act as if I had it all together and hide that I was dying on the inside.

By the time I was 19 years old, I was forced to figure out where and how to live on my own. I was kicked out of my home, because I had decided to follow my belief in God and my calling to serve others – one my family did not support. I had no money, home, food, or family. At that time, I focused on the situation at hand and how to keep moving forward. I didn't look towards tomorrow – but only at the present moment – and pressed on. I found ways to support myself, in order to get to Miami University, by working four jobs and staying with friends. The pressure was building and at times, I was very tired and found ways to cope via overachieving. This distracted me from knowing my true being - until I was finally still enough to face the deep sadness and pain. I strived to capture my thoughts and believe what was good in order to move forward in love, peace and joy.

Through all the years, I grew in choosing to tell myself what was true about me on the inside. This would be my saving grace and would arm me with intense emotional intelligence and awareness. It would be the good that would come from all the torture. As a result of being under constant attack by the people who should have loved and protected me the most, I learned how to go to a deep space of forgiveness, love, and acceptance... but also accountability. My path to this choice came about over several years, when I worked hard to focus on what my voices were saying to me, and then what I wanted to change regarding myself. I asked for help from those I trusted, and who had gone ahead of me, living life joyfully and compassionately in the moment. I found that not focusing on the perpetrators, but on how I was responding really healed my heart and mind. This was an intense repeated choice, yet my deepest point of growth.

Bolstering me- I found the love of riding and racing my bike, providing me freedom to be a kid, the adoration I have for nature and the camaraderie of friends who became like family. I spent up to 15 hours a week training with my coach and team for several years. I discovered that I had great strength, skill, dedication and a place again to practice overcoming fear.

I grew in courage every time I faced the line and raced shoulder to shoulder on technical concrete courses. I realized that I already knew how to face fear and win. I had done this since I was a young child. Now I realize that it is the good that came out of my development—where I now win at life, work, and as a competitive cyclist by being intensely aware of my thoughts, beliefs and the limitless choices in life. The view that there are always options freed me to take in more joy and peace.

In the last two plus years, I divorced, moved into my own home, sent my children off to school after homeschooling them for eight years. I also started to work outside of the home and to prepare a new life. In this transition time, I also had a traumatic, near-death accident.

During my national criterium cycling race in June of 2013, I was ready to place on the podium. I had been training all winter and told myself that I would be really strong this year. Although this was not my "A" race, I was feeling joyful and smiling even when my lungs and legs burned. I had learned to keep pushing no matter how I felt (great in life too), and filled with a balance, wisdom and courage. Today would be no different. With 52 racers of all ages packed together, we took sharp turns at 30 mph, with zigs and zags and the thoughts of winning. As we went into our last three laps, somehow I was trapped and bumped which sent me suddenly to the pavement where my head and neck hit the curb. My entire right side took the fall. I do not remember any of this. I apparently convulsed as race doctors came running to help me. I was quickly taken to a hospital 20 minutes away while calls came in from the paramedics that I was not going to live. My ex-husband and children were notified.

Upon my arrival, doctors worked quickly as my body was crushed on the right side. My skull was cracked open, my temporal bone was broken, nine of my ribs were crushed, a lung was punctured, and my shoulder was separated.

The doctors put me in a medically induced coma on life support and checked on me every hour to see if my brain would ever support my life again. For days, my friends and family prayed and sang for me. About eight days in, I had my back cut open during surgery to plate my nine ribs, which created a lung cage again.

The doctors were amazed and astonished when I was able to fight for my life like they had never seen before. They told my friends that it was because of my strength that I survived and that most people in my situation in ICU would have died.

I credit my survival to two factors: first, it was an answer to the prayers of many; and second, it was my will to keep going. My body and mind had already known adversity, and they remembered how to keep moving. I was not going to give up.

In spite of the many barriers I have faced in my life –pain, trauma and loneliness–I have achieved many things:

- Awarded leader of my school at age 8
- 1st chair violinist/concert mistress in an orchestra of at least 25 violinists
- Competitive track runner
- Vocalist and music leader
- Motivational speaker
- A degree from Miami University (OH)
- Graduate school work
- President's Club in sales
- National recognition in Fox National and Local News, Crain's Chicago Business, The Chicago Tribune, 190 N. T.V. etc., for my ability to start up a successful business with revenues of over a million dollars within the first six months
- National competitive cyclist ranked 2 out of 998 my first year of racing in 2011

Most importantly, what I have realized is that I have become strong and happy by just being myself and not anyone else! I have learned not to waiver based on what other people think or say about me. This is what I had to accomplish. I would have died emotionally and mentally, if I had listened to the harsh abusive words of my mother.

I choose to believe what I know is true about myself and let that be my guide: to be still and know that I am created like no other, for a purpose that only I can fulfill at this moment. To know that I only have now – the past is gone and the future is not guaranteed.

I have the power to think and then to believe, making that my reality… and no one can take that away. We all have this power. This courage breeds more courage deep within the soul and loving oneself deeply spills over to loving others. The power is in choosing and aligning with who we are, not what we do. This brings healing, peace and joy. We are made to be and live fully; the doing comes alongside and matches up to who we are, if we are mindfully aware.

Just as the brain has the ability to take away a life, it also has the power to give back beyond what is expected. The power to be driven by the intrinsic and the ability to grow in my awareness of all the choices I have from major to minor each day (the repetitive practice of this and not living in fear) has caused me to live courageously, passionately, and kindly, while also loving who I am.

It also gives me comfort to know that I am overseen and cared for by God and the Creator of the Universe who always wants the best for me. In spite of my smallness and tiny brain, I trust in Him. I long for others to seek their called, unique being and go after what they most likely already know is their truth within themselves.

My dedicated work now in my coaching practice is to help others return to listening and honoring their inner voice and teaching them how to build up their inner self, in order to go after what they hear.

The joy of knowing that no one can take away my thinking and that the impact of what I tell myself is all mine is the source of a life lived on purpose. My coaching practice honors those who want to make a difference first to themselves, in order to leave a legacy behind to those who matter most to them, whether at work or in life.

If there is more to you and your business of life, and you want to be filled with joy no matter the pain and uncertainty of this life, choose with care.

My Focus in a Day:

1.  Before I put my feet to the ground in the morning, I am still and give thanks. I ask God to help me love Him with all my heart, mind, soul, and strength, and to help me love my neighbor as I love myself. I

really think through what I am saying, since this is a really deep and new experience each moment.

2.  Work out: I stretch before I leave my room, breathe deeply 3 times, and exercise my arms. I ride my bike for 1 to 3 hours a day or run one time a week. I work hard at work – to be my best to do my best.

3.  Eat really green and organic as much as possible. Since I was a young child, I haven't consumed animals. I cook almost all of my foods, so I know what's in them. I also enjoy creating new meals! I like to be mindful of what I eat.

4.  Pray with my children in the morning, read with them, pray before bed, and maybe sing with them too. I help them realize what they want in life and show them how to get there.

5.  Make sure I read in order to keep growing and learning. I read the Bible to study how others have grown and overcome adversity. I love reading biographies to learn about others who have achieved something similar to what I want in my life. When I follow them, I learn from them – I do this in becoming a top cyclist as well.

6.  Live Right Now: I am thankful for what I have now and tell myself that my family and I have all that we need right now, and we are fine. I live each moment to the fullest and with joy. I am really aware of my thoughts and my focus. I tell myself what is good and true, and cast worry aside. I listen to my inner self and follow my intuition.

7.  Get outside every day and look for the beauty in nature. When I become stressed or overwhelmed, this calms me.

8.  Laugh and enjoy friends: I share life with my dear friends by making time to talk and spend time with them. We are silly at times, we support one another, and I am real with them. I wisely choose the people that I will be close to, and we make memories together.

9.  Journal: I journal my thoughts, desires, needs, concerns, and

prayers. This has been going on for over twenty years, and I find that my mind rests easier when I put my thoughts on paper, instead of holding it all in. I can also look back later at all the neat things that have occurred in my life.

10. BE ME-Creative and Unique- and love being me more and more- HOLD COURAGE- and Keep Moving Forward!

Blessings to you and thanks to my God! If you are moved to be your fullest unique self – living in joy- even if there is pain, difficulties, loss and stress- please connect with me via my email at: debrasunderland3@gmail. com. for a complimentary 45 minute session to see how we may work together and focus on your chosen life and work. Live in this moment.

# Debra Sunderland

## LIVE This Day on Purpose While Aligning Your Being and Doing

Debra Sunderland is a motivational speaker / leadership coach and entrepreneur who has been featured in several Chicago periodicals such as The Chicago Tribune, and Crain's Chicago Business, as well as on Fox National News and 190 North T.V., for her ability to achieve explosive growth and peak performance in sales and marketing within her own company as well as for corporations and start-up businesses. Debra now turns her award winning coaching strategies to help people achieve what she personally has been able to achieve not only in business, but also in life. Some of the tools that Debra integrates to achieve results focus on the alignment of the body, mind and soul. Living a holistic approach to wellness of the body, via daily spiritual centering, mind awareness, exercise and vegetarian-vegan eating for over thirty years, she also has succeeded as a nationally ranked cyclist. Debra believes that her athletic training and competitive racing can be applied to all aspects of life. This includes motivating and guiding those, who desire their own growth in achieving their life's calling and purpose. "In the racing around and doing of life, we tend to lose our true, unique being. Our being must come first, in order for the ultimate impact of our doing to shine with lasting joy and peace. Our work and life best come forth when they are aligned. My coaching is integral and brings together the unique purpose of your life."

Connect with me - I would love to work with you!

Debra Sunderland
Sunderland Coaching, LLC
Certified Corporate Goal Coach
22 Indian Drive
Clarendon Hills, IL 60514
708-989-1159
debrasunderland3@gmail.com
www.DebraSunderland.com

# Valerie Janke
## *Finding Balance through Strength*

This book is about strength… In this chapter, you will read about both physical and emotional strength. You will read about catharsis and personal development and, hopefully, you will be inspired. I am a sum of many parts, a 20 year veteran of the Financial Services Industry, recent college graduate (after 21 years of avoiding degree completion), a daughter and sister, a recently separated married woman and a Figure Bodybuilding Competitor who has qualified for National Level competition in the National Physique Committee's Bodybuilding Federation (NPC). So, you could say there's been some stuff going on. When Christie Ruffino asked me to participate in this book, I was flattered. And, a little embarrassed. I have never taken compliments very well. The reason this has been written is that if my story helps just one person, then the exercise was a success.

Let's start with the bodybuilding, since that is what Christie asked me to focus on. Since I was geeky, small, insecure and sometimes socially awkward, I was never a physically fit kid. Diagnosed with Type I Diabetes at the age of 6, most people assumed I would never be able to be physically active. At the time (1974), the prognosis wasn't a very positive one. Being told at that time to expect to be on a second kidney transplant in your mid-40's, with a realistic life expectancy of 53 has an impact on a 6 year old. None of that has been the case. But a second cousin of mine did not fare as well and died after a third kidney was rejected and she developed cancer due to anti-rejection medication as a result of her Diabetes. She was 58. 40 years ago, treatment protocols were not what they are today, so a complication developed. It is a condition best described as asymptomatic low blood glucose. It means not knowing that your glucose levels are dangerously low and that you may pass out suddenly. This condition made being physically active problematic. Prior to insulin pump therapy being the "go to" treatment option for people with Type 1, it could be dangerous to be too active. I finally got on an insulin pump about 14 years ago. It was life changing! With glucose levels stabilizing, my energy level increased. Feeling bad for all those years and not realizing it, it was amazing to feel good. For the first time, there was a mechanism to help me be active and physically strong. I joined a Bally's Total Fitness.

At first, there was a lot of cardiovascular work. My mother had her first heart attack at 43 and my Type 2 diabetic grandfather on my mother's side died at 56 while having his second bypass surgery. Following in their footsteps was not the plan. I lost a little weight and started to sleep and eat better. Those glucose levels improved further. Then, as happens to all of us who begin an exercise regimen, I hit a plateau. A benefit that I had not taken advantage of came with the new health club membership; a one on one session with a personal trainer. I scheduled a session with her. She was an Exercise Physiology major at the University of Chicago and a very smart woman. She took me through a workout and taught me some things. She told me that weight training builds muscle and that having more muscle mass makes people burn calories more efficiently. I learned that I enjoyed weight training and that it also helped women who were approaching middle age maintain bone density. She also said that women (for the most part anyway) don't get big muscles, no matter how hard they train, so I didn't have to worry about "bulking up". In retrospect, that's incredibly funny now. Weight training was added to my regular workout schedule. I found myself getting leaner and stronger! I began to experience the best glucose control of my life.

Then, it happened again. That dreaded PLATEAU! It was frustrating to say the least. That same week something life altering happened. My company posted a story on its internal site about a woman in another office who competed in Figure Bodybuilding. I read the story and immediately called her, but got her voicemail. She called me back and had me on the phone for an hour. When we were done with that conversation, I was committed to doing my first "show". She shared with me that her personal mission was to encourage people to lead a healthy, fit and active lifestyle. It was a path that I chose to be on. That was some 11 or 12 years ago. We are still in touch with each other and continue to cheer for each other. Every day should be a celebration, right? Into training I went. We talked often and inspired each other to continue muscle and personal development. We sent each other pictures of our progress. I hired that trainer to get me through it. She also knew people who competed and was a power lifting competitor herself. The people at Bally's worked out with me. Once the story leaked, a group of people surrounded me who supported my goal. One learns a lot the first time through contest preparation. You learn about the lengths that you are willing to go to accomplish a goal. I never really tried hard for most things until then.

I found out quickly (after lackluster results in my first contest), that I don't build muscle easily. In fact, it's very, very difficult for me. I also found that my diabetic kidneys don't like protein shakes! So, to build and protect, I have to balance proper whole food nutrition and a workout schedule that targets and focuses on certain muscle groups each day. That all came through time and trial… and error! But, the only time we truly fail is if we fail to try. A lifetime with a scary prognosis changes you. You learn to go all out for things that you choose to do.

My colleague became more than just a friend, she became my coach. She and her husband worked with me remotely for a few years. This period included my first sports related injury, kidney issues and being told by someone else's coach that I didn't have enough muscle. We tried and failed and tried again. Finally, I asked one of the show promoters what I was doing wrong. He said that my posing was a little off, that my limbs were long and too thin, but that I was probably doing nothing wrong. He suggested a new coach who lived in my state. She was more hands on… I was a secret fan of hers since I saw her compete at one of my first shows. That's when things began to change.

She tapped into places in my body and my head that were holding me back. Contest preparation is always a cathartic process. I learned early in the process that if you push yourself harder than even you thought you could in pursuit of a goal, a fire inside of you starts to burn. I learned that I have control of my surroundings, my food, my workouts and that I like that. When I found my next coach, I learned this… that I have to have balance. Balance. Nothing more. To truly excel in this sport, or really anything in life, balance is the key.

**(I'm in the middle)**

I competed on a team for the first time. There were teammates to talk to who were going through the same things. The sense of camaraderie was inspiring. I started to find the balance that I sorely needed. My first show with my new coach qualified me for Nationals. What a tremendous and somewhat stunning experience! No one, ever in my life, had given me credit for being physically strong and there I was a Nationally Qualified Physique Competitor! However, a better person also stood there with that trophy. A woman who was more empathetic, a better friend, a better leader and an emotionally stronger person was on that stage that night. I competed as part of this coach's team for the entire 2007 and 2008 seasons.

At a show in late 2008, there was a judge who worked at a gym that had a team competing. Some of the competitors were unfairly placed that day. The consensus from coaches, audience and other judges was for another national qualification. That was not the result. My coach and I talked. She wanted me to stay with her and compete again the following season but enter as an individual competitor. It's a cathartic moment when you realize what you will NOT do, and I wouldn't do that. Should one go around the system for one's own personal gain? I left the sport for 6 years. I completed my Bachelor's program (Summa Cum Laude) at 42 years old and focused on other areas of my life for a while.

Fast forward to 2014. Do you know that feeling you get when something is missing from your life? Was that a lack of balance reemerging? When my mother had her emergency triple bypass that January, I was already considering going back to bodybuilding. The camaraderie, control, challenges and the balance that the physical aspects of training provided were missing from my life. The physical provided balance to the intellectual and professional. However, with the responsibilities of helping mom recover, the time commitment was impossible. Life had taken some turns over the last few years. Some of the changes included a disengaged marriage, an enormous career shift and less than stellar glucose control. I began working with an awesome business coach who was helping me rediscover my inner rock star. I had begun to surround myself with positive, encouraging people. After a long break and with mom beginning to feel better, I started training in August of 2014 and did my first show in November.

As always, the lessons came. It was time to be in control of my own feelings, attitudes and energy. The challenge helped me to find my own feet again in a world that I had allowed to control me. It was with clearly defined goals that I traveled my path: not finishing last, nailing those poses and coming in at the same conditioning as 6 years ago. The poses were perfect (it was like riding a bicycle after all). I finished 14th out of 17 in my category and my conditioning was only slightly below that of 6 years ago (at 47 it was all good). It was a happy and satisfying experience.

It felt great to feel good about myself again; to stretch and do something a little bit terrifying. The balance, control and clarity came back. There were things that were missing for years that I didn't know were missing at all. That persona that we all have hiding within showed herself. The inner rock star that my business coach knew was there and that my bodybuilding coach (who took me back after such a long time) did as well. It was the one that my best friend could see, my business partner could see and my colleagues could see, but I could not.

As I said in my introduction to this chapter, I have many facets. Figure Bodybuilder is only one of them. To be closer to complete than in the past is the real accomplishment. Competing is a way to dig deep into yourself and to find your inner strength. You can learn from your experiences and get back in touch with the things that drive you. My mother hates it! She thinks that I get too thin and that I don't look healthy. By way of explanation I said "Mom, this is my way of challenging myself. I learn something new each time that I do this and I do it for no one but me." This time, she finally understood. It wasn't long after my last show that I found a new place to live and a new inner peace. My business coach commented earlier in 2014 that she saw in me someone ready to move. Now, I'm there; emotionally stronger, more focused and on top of my game. My mom was over at my place recently and told me that I looked better than she'd seen me in years. I was finally "back". Bodybuilding is my thing. Find your thing, whatever it may be (meditation, exercise, cooking classes, reading…) and find your special place that is all about you. Do that, and it will change you forever.

# Valerie Janke

Valerie Janke is a 20 year Financial Services Industry professional. She is an active member of her local community, serving on the Lisle Area Chamber of Commerce Ambassador and Dinner Dance Committees. She actively volunteers at Lisle Eyes to the Skies and with JDRF Illinois as a Family Mentor and Outreach Committee member, helping the families of people who are newly diagnosed with Type 1 Diabetes. She is the Membership Director for The Financial Planning Association of Illinois, Inc. and also serves on their Communications Committee. She has participated in "Age Well DuPage" and "Financial Planning Day". And, finally, she is the Treasurer for Australian Shepherd Rescue Midwest, Inc. Her volunteer efforts are tireless.

She is a professional who is dedicated to helping people achieve their goals and live fuller, better lives. Some of her professional efforts include outreach and education. She strives to have a positive impact on the lives of those around her, be they K9 or humans. She is a physique competitor and regularly runs 5K races as well as obstacle course runs. Her favorites include Zombie Runs since she prefers to be chased when running.

Valerie Janke
1100 E. Warrenville Road, Suite 100
Naperville, IL 60532
331-229-4038
773-852-6094
vjanke@wradvisors.com
www.linkedin.com/pub/valerie-janke-cfp

# Dr. Emily Loveland
## *Make Wellness Your Reality*

Ever since I can remember, my weight has been up and down. Mostly up. And up and up in the past few years. I was never overly concerned about my weight because I've always been "relatively healthy". I have a career that I love. I run a chiropractic practice that is lovely, busy and profitable. I have an active social life. I have an amazing family and an abundance of life-long friends. I'm happy. And seemingly healthy.... Until I wasn't.

About 3 years ago, I began to notice some itchy patches on the soft part of my left elbow. It would come and go, maybe once or twice a year, then a bit more frequently, and lasted longer, and then it spread to my chest. It became intolerable and felt like my skin was on fire from within. I couldn't sleep because I was up all night itching. It was affecting my work and my sanity. I went to urgent care, where I was given a diagnosis of eczema and a strong steroid medication. Within 2 days, my skin was calm and healing. Great! I finished a two week course of the medication and thought all was well. Within a day of coming off the medication, my skin erupted again with a vengeance. Thus began a vicious cycle of flare-ups and steroids, with no reprieve. So there I was, significantly over-weight and now unhealthy.

Over the years I tried many diets. Most of them were extreme, unhealthy and resulted in me giving up and going back to eating comfort food, junk food, convenience food or foods that were inevitably making me ill. I am a health care practitioner that dispenses advice about well-being, yet I found it impossible to apply the ideas of healthy living to my own life. But this story is not about losing weight, it's about gaining health.

For me, being reliant on medications is no way to live, especially after discovering that making dietary changes could reverse my condition. I knew I needed to make a change. My medical physician was great for making the flares go away, but it was my desire to use self-healing and natural medicine that opened my eyes to overcome MEDIOCRE health.

I made an appointment with a natural medicine chiropractic doctor. She began by ordering routine blood work to evaluate my health status. My blood work was normal, except the eosinophils levels were elevated which can indicate an allergic reaction. She then performed food sensitivity testing revealing that my body was over-reacting to many foods. She explained that my skin flares were a symptom of an unhealthy gut that was not digesting foods correctly. I began treating myself with supplementation and a major overhaul of food choices. The process is not fast, but the flares are becoming less severe with less need for prescription medication.

I was hesitant to share this story because I didn't want to have my picture taken. I am far from being at my ideal weight, but then I thought about it, and realized this book is not about being perfect; it's about progress and inspiration! When we put food into our mouth, we are making a choice to slowly poison our body or to nourish and heal it. There are so many medical conditions that can be eliminated, minimized or avoided by making simple changes. Diabetes, high blood pressure, high cholesterol, thyroid dysfunction, acid reflux, irritable bowel syndrome, auto-immune diseases, etc., are all influenced by diet. There is not one diet for everyone, so I encourage you to find a naturally practicing MD, chiropractor, acupuncturist, naturopath, or health coach. They are trained to help you get well, not just cover up symptoms.

In the meantime, please consider the foods you eat and implement some simple changes that could significantly improve your health and well-being:

1. Eat whole foods- Mostly vegetables, some fruits, lean proteins, nuts, seeds and ancient grains like quinoa. Gluten is out! Processed foods are out! Fast food is out! Sugar is out! Dairy is not the best

choice, so limit it for sure. Don't leave your food to chance. Not being prepared is a recipe for disaster. It is not as important to count calories as it is to count chemicals. Real food does not have a mile long ingredient list.

2.  Drink water! Half of your body weight in ounces is preferable. Do this every day. Soda pop is not water, tea is not water, and coffee is not water. Water is water. Conditions like arthritis, tendonitis, and bursitis are often due to dehydration, so drink up!

3.  Exercise! Find an activity that you love and do it! Move your body at least 30 minutes every day. Strength and flexibility are so important, especially as we age.

4.  Take quality supplements. Everyone can benefit from a multivitamin, Omega 3, probiotic and Vitamin D supplement. You should not be taking handfuls of supplements unless you are working with a health care practitioner for correcting deficiencies. Get your nutrition from your food first. Supplements are just that, supplements to a healthy and nourishing diet! Physician grade supplements are the best choice to ensure you are getting the most absorbable form.

Making these changes may not be easy at first. If you are anything like me, I had to change a lifetime of bad habits. My most long term success has come from tackling one habit at a time. I started with eliminating gluten, since it was my most severe skin flare trigger. I then moved onto dairy, exercise and so on. I have adopted the motto that food is not a reward or a punishment; it is the fuel to keep me running. I enjoy veggies. I have found so many wonderful recipes that satisfy my senses. Get creative. I make a butternut squash and green apple soup that would knock your socks off, a non-dairy "cheese" sauce that is out of this world, and a mint green smoothie that tastes just like a mint chip chocolate shake!

Twice a year, I also give my body an internal break by doing a gentle 10 day detox. Detoxing is a great way to clear out the toxins, break through plateaus, and reset the liver and gut. We are exposed to many daily toxins from our foods, cleaning products, and the environment. The detox program that I have chosen allows me to eat veggies, fruits and legumes along with taking 3 supportive supplements that are loaded with anti-oxidants and super foods. Let me get on my soap box about detox programs for a moment. Detox programs often are associated with a number, 3 days, 10 days, 30 days... I often hear people abuse detox programs (in the past I've done it too). They restrict their diet so severely, they starve themselves, or drink crazy concoctions in the hopes of losing a few pounds, then when the "X" amount of days are over they gorge on junky foods. That is not how a detox should work. A detox should be a gentle reprieve to reset your systems, lift brain fog and encourage the continuation of eating healthy foods. Clean eating does not have an end date!

Don't let cheats, vacations, or social events permanently de-rail your progress. I get it, life happens. There are times when eating a piece of cake is mandatory. I've found that when I'm faced with "cake", I now take a smaller piece, or just take a bite, and sometimes I even say no thank-you. By cleaning up my diet, my taste palate has changed and often cheating with junk foods can make me feel lousy. Saying no to junky foods is way more appealing than feeling bloated, headachy, or having a skin flare up.

Finally, there are a million excuses to eating poorly. "I'm too tired to cook" "I'm too busy to exercise" "I love bread too much". Trust me, I've used them all. But believe this, making the changes has saved my life and is restoring my health. Taking medication and putting on the pounds is not part of the natural aging process. I hope you make the decision to take charge of your health and make wellness your reality!

*"All good is hard. All evil is easy. Dying, losing, cheating, and mediocrity is easy. Stay away from easy."* – Scott Alexander

Health & Happiness,

Dr. Emily

# Dr. Emily Loveland

Dr. Emily Loveland, Chiropractic Physician began her collegiate career at Grand Valley State University just outside of Grand Rapids, MI were she received a Bachelor's of Science degree in 2000. While at GVSU, she completed the athletic training program which qualified her to sit for the National Athletic Trainer's Examination. For the next two years, she provided health care services, as the head athletic trainer, to the student/athletes of a high school in Indiana. In June 2002, Dr. Loveland completed massage therapy training at the Midwest Academy of Healing Arts in Brownsburg, IN.

Dr. Loveland received a Doctorate of Chiropractic degree from the National University of Health Sciences in 2006. While attending chiropractic school, she received certifications to perform acupuncture, Graston technique, and Kinesiotaping. She has also attended numerous continuing education courses in exercise rehabilitation and nutritional therapies.

In 2009, Dr. Loveland went into private practice in the quaint town of St. Charles, IL, combining traditional chiropractic therapies, massage and acupuncture in a beautiful spa setting. Her treatment style is unique, coining the term "touch diagnostics". Dr. Loveland prides herself on providing her patients with compassionate, individualized, hands-on care that focuses on the wellness of the body, not just treatment of the symptoms.

Dr. Loveland added adjunct professor to her achievements in 2014, when asked to share her passion for education and healing at the local community college. She teaches Anatomy & Physiology for future massage therapists. She considers it a great honor to lead students to becoming great body workers.

Dr. Emily Loveland is a breath of fresh air to the medical community, offering no-nonsense treatment plans that are respectful of her patients' time and finances. She is a big fan of self-care options, encouraging patient's to take charge of their own health with food choices, exercise and stress management strategies that can be followed in their day to day life to keep them well. Just walking into her office offers a feeling of peace and tranquility.

Dr. Emily Loveland, DC
Tranquility Spa & Wellness Center
113 N. Second Ave
St. Charles, IL 60174
630-762-9864
drloveland@relaxattranquility.com
www.RelaxatTranquility.com
www.CleanBurnShape.com/partner/70177

# Michele Saxman
## *The Secret*

I was given the book, *The Secret* written by Rhonda Byrne, by a friend in June 2008 during a particularly bad time in my life. She told me to write my name and the date I received it on the first page of the book under the other signatures. After I read it, if I believed what the book said, I was to pass it on to someone else that I felt was having a rough time and needed help. This new person was supposed to write their name and receipt date under my name. After reading the book, they could either give it back or pass it on to someone that they felt needed help. This was the third time that she had started sending *The Secret* on its way. She was sure *The Secret* could help me sort out my problems. And it did!

Over the years, when I am having an especially difficult time in my life, I re-read *The Secret*. After reading *The Secret,* I find whatever in my life that is so troubling starts to work its way out. *The Secret* is a spiritual, faith-based, optimistic, self-help book. It helps you to get back your "mojo" and to start believing in yourself again. Let me tell you about my adventures with *The Secret.*

This friend and I met at a weight loss clinic in Bloomingdale, IL. She was finishing her journey and I was starting mine. She had gone through a divorce a few years earlier and I was just starting my divorce. This weight loss clinic was very different from others – it was for women only. It was just what I needed. It was a place where I could come to complain, cry, tell my story, and receive sympathy and sisterly love while losing weight.

The previous two years had been very tumultuous and difficult for me.

In 2006, my husband met a woman he wanted to be more than a girlfriend. He had many girlfriends before, but he wanted to stay with this one. This was very, very difficult for me since we had been married in college and had run a company for 20 years. We were together for 28 years and more or less grew up together. Now what was I to do?

In April 2007, I found out that my daughter was to have a baby in May. I had not heard from her for 9 months. I was ecstatic – I was going to be a grandmother!!! However, being a grandmother was not going to be so easy. She was living in a drug rehabilitation center in Elgin, IL. The owner wanted her to stay there and for me not to be involved with her or my grandson. In July, my daughter thought it was best for her and my 6-week old grandson to come live with me in Carol Stream, IL. That was one of the happiest days of my life!! My husband (who was still around), daughter and I settled into life with a new baby for the next year.

In April 2008 it became clear to my husband and me, that he wanted to move on with his girlfriend. In June we separated and in August the divorce started.

This is when I first received *The Secret*. I had to re-read paragraphs several times to understand them. I found that it was very interesting. I had a friend going through a similar situation and sent the book to her after I read it. I didn't quite know what to make of the book, although, I would soon find out.

In September 2008, because of her drug problems, I asked my daughter to leave without her son. By October, I was running the company by myself and raising my 1-year-old grandson at the age of 49. I was on my own for the first time since leaving home for college. My body, mind and spirit needed help.

Instead of focusing on the negative, I want to focus on the positive things that took place during that time. At the beginning of this story (January 2008), I knew that it was time to look and feel better. I was getting tired of working 60 hours a week and 10 to 12 hours a day. I would go to a restaurant to wind down and eat because I was too tired to cook. I was heavier than ever before (60 lbs. over my pregnancy weight). I just couldn't stand myself any longer. I am sure that in the back of my mind, I thought if I slimmed down I could keep my husband.

As a result, I joined the weight loss clinic. I believed there was no way that the soft physical activity and changes in food preparation would help me lose weight. However, I kept at it. With the friendship and help of the women at the clinic and with God's guidance, I lost weight and felt much better.

I met a travelling salesman in February 2008 who made me feel good about myself. He made me feel important and gave me the feeling that I could move on with my life without being married.

At the time of the separation in June 2008, my husband also separated from the company. I kept the house, the company and the debt while he moved in with his mom in Oak Brook, IL and his girlfriend in Detroit – laying the groundwork to start a new company that would be competing with mine.

I kept all of the customers and the manufacturers were still with me. My old babysitter was ecstatic that she had another baby to watch after raising my daughter from 6 weeks of age. I no longer fretted about my husband being with girlfriends. I had moved on. Everything was looking rosy.

In June, I also noticed a 20 pound weight loss. I was dating a very nice looking gentleman and met a great guy at a Carol Stream Chamber of Commerce golf outing. Yes, men seemed to be noticing me. I was feeling good about myself and it was showing in my increased confidence.

During the next few months, everything stayed about the same. By the end of 2008, I had lost 30 lbs. and felt great. However, I was feeling the emptiness of not having a companion. I was also tired of the bar scene and was getting too old for that anyway.

I gave my first *The Secret* book away (right after I read it) to someone who I knew needed help. I went out and bought *The Secret* again in October

2008. I put my name and date on the first page just like the last time. I went back and read it again. This time I learned that you had to make room for what you want. You have to get ready for it to come your way. How did this help in finding a companion? I decided to stop spreading my clothes out in my walk-in closet to take up all the space where my husband's clothes used to be (very silly looking). I put my clothes back in my half of the closet and left the other half open for the new man to come into my life.

In February 2009, the Carol Stream Chamber of Commerce had a cruise to Mexico – about 50 members strong. I had never been on a cruise. I was very involved with the Chamber. I was even an ambassador. What the heck. I started thinking romantically about all the cruise movies I had seen with women finding their husbands on cruises. I signed up.

One week before I went on the cruise, I met a man. He is a man who has so totally filled my emptiness that he has remained my companion for 7 years now. He helped raise my grandson and without a whimper went back to changing diapers at 49.

Before reading *The Secret,* I always considered myself lucky. Whenever I concentrated hard enough on winning something, I won. As an example, during an assembly in high school I wanted to be called on stage. I concentrated hard and was picked. My bank was giving away a baseball signed by Andre Dawson and I won. A business raffle was giving away Sox tickets. I won. I knew that I was going to win a forklift quote for the country of Albania against the biggest manufacturers - and I did.

Even before reading *The Secret,* I had already been using it for small items.

Reading *The Secret,* reminded me of the joke: *The river overflowed causing flooding in the street. A man walked out of his house and saw water up to his porch. He looked up to the heavens and said, "God, please save me from this flooding." His neighbor came by in the car and said, "We'd better leave before the flooding gets really bad." "No, thank you. God will provide." The waters were past the first floor of the house. The city police came by in a row boat. "We are rescuing those left to higher ground." "No, thank you. God will provide." They continued rowing. The man was now on his roof because the waters were up to the second floor. The coast guard came by in a helicopter. "We are rescuing those left to higher ground." He answered, "No, thank you. God will provide." They continued flying. The waters finally engulfed the man. Once in heaven in front of God, the man protested, "My faith was such I thought you would rescue me from the flooding waters." God answered, "Who do you think provided the neighbor in the car, the police in the rowboat and the Coast Guard in the helicopter?"*

After reading *The Secret* the second time, I understood it a bit more. I stopped asking God to NOT let certain things happen and started to ask for what I wanted to happen and looked for ways to make it happen.

Was it because of the recession, my ex-husband taking all my customers or the court demanding I give up my company or my grandson? (I chose my grandson.) Or was it God's hand moving me in a different direction?

At this same time, my boyfriend thought it best for us to move out of the Carol Stream area. Therefore, my grandson and I moved to Brookfield, IL. We found the cutest little house with a nice backyard 4 blocks from schools and lots of children his age to play with.

I met new friends, found out what I missed working like a maniac while raising my daughter, started volunteering at school and church and coaching sports to young children. It was a totally different life and I loved it!!!! I realized that during the last 20 years, I had lost my identity in the identity of my company. I made a lot of new friends who liked me for being myself.

God works in mysterious ways. In November 2012, we were no longer raising my grandson. A few months after this happened, the Akita Rescue called me to see if I was still looking to rescue an Akita.

They had one that looked the same and had the temperament of my last rescued Akita who had gone to doggie heaven three years earlier. We rescued him.

After re-reading *The Secret* because I was in another "funk' in my life, everything started to turn around again. I stopped laying back waiting for whatever life brought me and started to go for what I wanted. I had put all the weight back on and then some, was feeling an emptiness where the need to work/do something with myself rested and generally needed to get back into the business world. I also retained the friendship of my previous customers and dealers and have started my company back up with their help.

I was out of work for about 3 years while raising my grandson. After we were no longer raising him, a friend helped me get a job at her company. The seasonal work ended just in time so that I could be involved in my church's Vacation Bible School Week. I helped with the children's games.

After working for the seasonal company and being laid off for the season, I found a job working with engineers selling material handling equipment. This made me want to get back into my company selling forklifts. I have started moving forward with the company, selling to both old and new customers.

I have (2) surrogate grandchildren that live close by and consider me like their grandmother, many more at Sunday School and coaching sports. I have three children and six grandchildren on my partner's side.

I no longer feel like I'm standing in cement – I am moving towards my goals again!!

I have been able to proceed with whatever it takes to talk to and see my grandson. As of this writing, I am able to talk to and see my grandson!!!

God has his ways and his own timeline for our life.

# Michele Saxman

Michele graduated from SIU-Carbondale with degrees in Electronic Technology and Business and has been the owner of Rapid Rentals & Sales, a forklift company, for over twenty years.

Michele has worked with people ranging from mechanics to small business owners to large companies and manufacturers around the world. In addition to working with English and German companies, she started the sideloader divisions of Fantuzzi USA (Italy) and Taylor Machine Works (Mississippi) and was one of the first Combilift (Ireland) dealers for the United States. Her company sold the largest reach stacker in the world. She has sold to many military installations in the United States, throughout North America, Hawaii, Puerto Rico and Albania

In her travels throughout North America and Europe, Michele has met many wonderful people and has always tried to be nice, fair and just to everyone including family, friends, acquaintances, passers-by, children and animals.

She is lucky to have a daughter and grandson as well as 3 children and 6 grandchildren on her partners' side. She also has a rescued dog, rescued cat, rescued turtle and fish.

Michele does volunteer work with children through coaching sports and teaching Sunday School. She considers herself blessed by the life she has had, her family and the people that she has met.

Michele Saxman
Rapid Rentals & Sales, Inc.
3229 Arthur Ave.
Brookfield, IL 60513
630-878-1310
rapdrentl@aol.com
www.Rapid-Rentals.com

# Kim Brondyke

## *My Journey to Become an Empowered Survivor*

Facebook has been a wonderful forum for life-affirming quotes. One of my favorites that resonates with me is this one: You don't know how strong you are until being strong is the only choice you have.

This is never more apt than when describing the path from childhood sexual abuse victim to survivor, which for me, was a lifetime journey. As a child, I was abused over a twelve-year period by people I knew – which is usually how it happens. That scary stranger who does bad things to you is an anomaly. It is more common for a child to be abused by someone they know and trust.

While I have never remembered all of it, I have also never forgotten or suppressed key scenes that stayed with me in a fog-like vise of a shameful movie that I produced and starred in. Psychologist Jean Piaget defines egocentrism, which appears in early childhood, as the inability to differentiate between the self and the other. So it was that I believed that the abuse perpetrated against me was actually orchestrated by me. I took on the responsibility of the evil done to me by others. This added to the shame that I already felt at being sexually abused.

**Something Worse than the Abuse**

When telling my story, I often say that the worst thing that happened to me was not the abuse. It is hard to believe, I know. When I was seven years old, someone close to me exhibited caring behavior that allowed me to let my guard down. I confided in this person and told them what was happening to me in an effort to understand it and be able to cope with it. I had no hope of actually stopping it. By then I thought I deserved it because I was bad. Unfortunately, this person – a member of my own family – did not offer me the safe haven for which I was hoping. Instead, I was overpowered, backed into a corner, accused of lying and threatened with being institutionalized should I ever repeat what I had just said.

It was a devastating experience that left me, at seven years old, believing that I was mentally ill. I never dared speak of the abuse again. The shame that I felt at being abused was magnified by the shame that I felt at being mentally ill (and branded a liar). A child never asks, "What did I do to deserve this?" Rather, a child draws unspoken conclusions that are, again, egocentric, and totally untrue. The child thinks, I deserve this because I am ugly or because I am bad. If I was pretty, smart, athletic – fill in the blank – this wouldn't be happening to me.

## The Worst Thing Turned Out to be the Best Thing

But I also tell others something else that's true as well. The worst thing that happened to me was also the best thing that happened to me. Had I not been told that I was mentally ill - and believed it - I would not have been proactive in my attempts to heal. Because I wanted nothing more than to be mentally healthy, I started counseling the first time when I was 18, even though back then – in the early '80s – people seeking counseling were stigmatized. To some degree, they still are.

Because of that stigma, as well as the stigma of being a victim, many survivors are not proactive in seeking help that they do not believe they deserve to begin with.

The road to emotional health and freedom is neither quick nor easy. For me, it has been a lifelong process that has affected my kids, impacted my marriage and, without the assistance of insurance, would have decimated my pocketbook. And that's the easy part. To talk about what happened is also not entirely difficult. What was so extremely brutal and scary was to face all the awful feelings that I had repressed when I was being victimized as a child.

In a perfect world, a child who experiences negative emotions due to trauma will have a safe adult to turn to in an effort to understand and process those emotions. Even in a fairly functional family, this is not often done as parents deal with the daily tasks of living that can be time consuming and, sometimes, overwhelming. This includes work, taking care of a home, getting the kids to school and helping them with their homework, making dinner, etc. All of these day-to-day responsibilities can cause even the best of parents to crowd out the emotional needs of a child. In a dysfunctional family, a child's emotional responses are not just ignored by the parents, but are also often ridiculed. "Don't be ridiculous." "What's wrong with you?" "You're crazy." "If you're that upset, why don't you just commit suicide?"

Therefore, the child learns to repress their feelings because they don't know how to handle them properly. This is what I did. I learned to "cut off" from my emotions and numb myself. The only emotions that I ever really allowed myself to feel were fear and anger – usually aimed at myself. I walked around in shock much like a person suffering from Post-Traumatic Stress Disorder, which many survivors do, in fact, suffer from.

Part of the healing process involves going back and feeling these awful emotions for the first time. At least it should. In standard talk therapy, you can talk for hours about what happened and yet never really feel it. I spent years in talk therapy coming into awareness about longstanding negative behavior patterns and family history, but never did any of it really heal the pain that I stuffed inside of me. I still carried considerable self-hate and suffered from depression, anxiety attacks and insomnia on a regular basis, although I lived an extremely healthy lifestyle as a runner and strength trainer.

**Making the Decision to be Happy was just the Beginning**

When I was 45 years old, I was sitting at the dinner table with my spouse and three children. After dinner, we were set to attend my oldest daughter's graduation from high school. I remember looking at her from across the table and realizing that I had spent 45 years being unhappy. I was deeply saddened as I realized that I had lived about half my life this way, and right then, I vowed to live the next 45 years being happy. I had only a small inkling of what that would involve, and no clue at all about how deep I would have to go to plumb the depth of emotions that I had buried in order to release myself from them!

Several months later, I changed counselors and started going to one that specialized in hypnotherapy. Hypnotherapy is a process that is less about what happened and more about how it felt. There were so many emotions that I had split off from, that it was a time consuming and tedious, but necessary, process that was also extremely painful – more painful than surgery. Having to go down that dark road and face those feelings squarely for the first time caused me to become suicidal twice during the most intense points in therapy. But the only way out is through, so it was all worth it. (Which, of course, is easy to say now that I am past it.) Finally facing the feelings and working through them, led me to the emotional strength and health that I had been looking for my entire life.

**You Did Right – You Survived!**

This is only my story, but I meet other survivors on a regular basis who inspire me with their stories of strength and bravery. I have met survivors who have risked being alienated from their families for speaking their truth. I have met survivors who have shared their story with the media in an effort to raise awareness. I have met survivors who have taken their abusers to court. But the biggest sign of strength is the survivor who gets up and decides to live another day. For a survivor, that is no small thing and can be the most difficult choice they make on an ongoing basis in their life. This is because for each survivor to live every day is a struggle.

In an older episode of Law and Order SVU, Detective Benson told a survivor, "You did right. You survived." That is great encouragement for a survivor, who instead often feels that they did something wrong simply because they are victims.

My life mission has become to help survivors to be proud and not ashamed, to see that they can move beyond survivor to thriver, to understand that while they will always carry the experience with them, they can move beyond it and even above it. I always tell people: God (in whatever form you know him to be) is no respecter of persons; what he gave to me he wants to give to everyone. Each of us is capable of having emotional health and freedom by the hard work we put into healing - NOT because someone else decides we deserve it.

I now know the truth and I'm committed to speaking it whenever I can: Every survivor has the inner strength already inside as well as the right to become an "Empowered Survivor."

# Kim Brondyke

Kim Brondyke, Certified Professional Coach (CPC), certified workshop facilitator and speaker, is the founder of The Empowered Survivor. She helps those who have experienced life-altering trauma find healing, empowerment and freedom. Her motivational approach and caring insight helps clients who are merely surviving day-to-day rather than thriving to reframe situations, overcome self-imposed roadblocks and uncover new solutions that foster lasting change. As a visionary and storyteller, Kim inspires others to transform and free themselves from traumatic experiences so they can live the life they want to live and not the life they were *told to live*. Through her work with victims of childhood abuse *and because of her own background of childhood sexual abuse,* she understands that everyone is surviving something. Through healing herself, she knows that you can only live your truth once you give voice to the truth of your experiences.

Kim was born and raised in the heart of the Midwest. After college, Kim spent nearly 20 years working in local, municipal and state government. Passionate about running and strength training, Kim became a personal trainer in 2008. It was during this time that she began to cultivate the coaching skills that she discovered within her after embracing the realization that change is always more effective if it starts from the inside out. Kim received her Certified Professional Coach certification through the Life Coach Institute, an organization accredited by the International Coaches Federation. Kim is a professional level member of Engaging Speakers and gives talks on empowerment and motivation.

Kim Brondyke
The Empowered Survivor
4724 Schwartz Avenue
Lisle, IL 60532
630-202-1986
kimbrondyke@gmail.com
www.TheEmpoweredSurvivor.com

# Noël Thelander
## *What's in Your Back Pocket?*

My favorite compliment from women who really know me, is this: *that I am a master at the art of reinventing myself and creating my own success.* Over the course of my adult life and career, I am grateful to have heard this more than once. It has been offered as a candid statement, not fished out at a low moment or in a request for feedback. It has been said in a way that tells me that I might have influenced someone else to make a positive life choice. My sister-in-law has told me that she uses my story as an example to her young women's group at church in order to help a new generation of women navigate their future family and career choices. An old friend faced with a relocation and career change told me that I had inspired her to bravely pursue a different area of expertise. In both cases, I felt encouraged and relieved to hear that my serial self-reinvention had been viewed positively by these women I admire because secretly I often worried that if I talked about my full range of business experience people would think I was making things up, or switching careers every week like the character in that 1980's TV show, Quantum Leap.

The truth is that I have had some uniquely intense career opportunities and have been able to place my confidence in a certain set of skills that have helped me succeed each time the outward career details changed. I've found that if you know yourself and understand the basic elements that make you unique or maybe even the best at something, you will recognize a good opportunity even when you were not looking for it. If you are truly blessed, you may someday find that even a wide range of seemingly disconnected experiences can eventually lead you to a surprisingly logical crossroads where everything happens to fit.

I don't know if I should be proud or embarrassed about this, but I have a history of taking on careers that I always perceived most other (possibly wiser) people would never consider. In these positions the expected results have been extremely demanding, the role itself usually slightly misunderstood, and the stakes have been high. I tend to walk right into challenges that encompass most people's greatest fears: public speaking, possible rejection, unpredictable outcomes, discussing death/taxes/money/weight gain, and hiring and firing people, to name a few. Yet I have learned, survived and succeeded at these with the support of great mentors, the memory of an elephant and a work ethic that helped me rise through the ranks quickly and then shift from proving myself individually to becoming a leader.

In college, I pursued a degree in psychology at a good university that I had picked for terrible reasons. A friend wanted to go there to follow her boyfriend, who gave us an impromptu tour that emphasized the Big 10 sports teams, classy historic buildings and social activities. It worked on me, so I applied, got in, picked my major and stuck with it even though I quickly discovered that this institution was not at all geared toward clinical (counseling) psychology, which I had thought about doing for as long as I could remember. I adapted and completed that unexpectedly research-oriented behavioral science degree, but also added a minor in journalism and loaded up on all available business and marketing courses for good measure.

Looking back, I was already following a healthy instinct toward self-reinvention. My creative response to unexpected change was a survival skill, and it had helped me prove myself, to myself. It felt right to have extra business concepts and communication abilities in my back pocket to help me deal with future twists and turns in my professional life.

After graduation, I was pleased to find a counseling position after all, where I provided group and individual behavioral counseling for weight loss center clients. It was a great first step in my career because I had to overcome the butterflies of public speaking, refine my listening and coaching skills, and use marketing savvy to influence positive change in my clients' lives. It was entry level pay but I was actually helping people, learning a lot and enjoying the work environment.

I found that I was interested in learning about the business itself and not just my role in it. I picked up on the demeanor and communication style of upper management, learned to track and focus on measurable performance goals, and discovered that I could relate well to a wide variety of social styles and group dynamics. I was promoted to my dream job, a collaborative training position that unfortunately was soon cut out of the company structure. However, these early career experiences were the first real mentoring that I had ever received and that resonated more with me than anything I had learned in an academic setting. After the training career path dried up, I gravitated to another 'marketing yet helping' field, the employment services / staffing industry.

In my new field, I was guiding the decisions of job seekers and hiring managers while ensuring that we operated the business skillfully and profitably. I developed sales, interviewing and matchmaking skills, took ownership of some major account relationships and even changed locations to become a branch manager for a team that included individuals who had been in the workforce much longer than I had. These challenging experiences helped me grow as a business person and in life. After I was married, we relocated twice for my career, once to California and once to Texas. For 15 years in this challenging industry, I was blessed to receive an abundance of wisdom, patience, brutal honesty and unflinching support from several exceptional mentors, some of whom were technically also my clients.

My responsibilities grew and I used my chameleon skills constantly, directing talented teams who operated large on-site staffing programs for our company's highest profile accounts. During these years, it felt like I lived two lives at once, or at least developed myself within two careers at once, for about

10 years straight. It was definitely a Quantum Leap feeling being employed by one big, successful corporation that gave me plenty of training, guidance, big scary goals and some tools for success. I also fully participated in the meetings and infrastructure of another big, successful corporation and worked in the client's facilities--first in biotech, then computer manufacturing and then international computer services. When it was done, I felt like I had gained about twenty years' experience in half that time. It was a decade-long double dose of how the world works and I was proud to have had the stamina to face the unique challenge of continually exceeding the expectations of two separate companies at once.

As my career and self-development progressed, so did my family life. It is an understatement to call parenthood a turning point, but going back to work as a new parent was the first time that my work/life boundaries were crystal clear to me. I wasn't willing to put in long hours or to do whatever it took to reach a company goal, because there was too much to lose (and the childcare people could be scary if you were one minute late). I became a time management ninja, walked away at the right time each afternoon, squeezed at-home follow up into the late evening/early morning hours and didn't act anxious or apologetic about being so schedule conscious. I was sure that this would put me on the 'mommy-track' where I'd be pigeonholed, underpaid and stuck on a plateau. It was still essential to have my data straight, my team running optimally and our key metrics showing a solid performance. I also had to be smarter about how I used my time. Surprisingly, my demeanor of calmness and clarity managed to set me apart from my more anxious, ego-driven peers. It was a happy surprise when I continued to move upward in responsibilities, pay grade and team recognition.

Based on that experience, I have tried to reassure other working moms when they feel stuck in the classic struggle to make a major career decision. We can all relate to that agonized soul searching where we seem haunted by the fact that we actually have available choices. In a 25-year career, I have worked under every kind of full time/part time/consulting scenario and can say with certainty that there is no ideal arrangement. But we are not going to fail our families no matter which alternative we choose.

Once we commit to a situation and build a routine around it, working moms can move mountains at home and at work. We can continue to excel professionally and personally without sacrificing one for the other. Having good mentors and power partners in your life--and always striving to be a good mentor or power partner--can be a remarkably stabilizing and strengthening force during times of self-reinvention, difficult life decisions or adapting to unexpected change.

Around the time that I went back to work as a new parent, my career was shifting away from a management role and into true leadership. In order to lead vs. manage, I had to define and achieve my own effectiveness by boosting the skills and effectiveness of a team, and by making sure that they had the resources to succeed. Being a superstar or the go-to person who always knew how to save the day was no longer included in this new definition of success. In fact, it could even be viewed as ineffectiveness. Highlighting the accomplishments of others, instilling tribal knowledge, and preventing and resolving difficulties were the kinds of details that suddenly deserved my time and attention. My best mentors from this career stage shared their timeless wisdom. Their voices still run through my mind sometimes, so I'll quote:

"I hired you for this job because I believe in you, I know you are good and I unconditionally support you. But please understand, I can be much better at supporting you if you share with me, early and often, what isn't working instead of all of the things we are doing well."

"In any meeting you attend, or consultation with a client, make a definite contribution by having an opinion, observation, recommendation or constructive criticism. We are paid to add value. Make every interaction better because you were there; and always tell people what you know they need, not what you think they want to hear."

"Build a business that works just as well when you are gone as it does when you are there. In fact, the goal is for it to run better when you stay out of the day-to-day details. But always know how to measure and explain your value and don't count on anyone else to do your PR for you."

These truisms came to mind again as I developed myself into one last new career four years ago. I am still educating and guiding clients in a specific aspect of their lives, now financial in nature. I am grateful for all of the experiences and mentoring that led me to my current role of Financial Advisor, which I love and feel blessed to be able to do for a living. I manage the strategic planning, investments and financial affairs of families and business owners to ensure that they reach their important, long term, quality-of-life financial goals.

Serving as a Financial Advisor turned out to be most like the therapist role that I had pictured for myself long ago. I am pleased to have reached a place in my career where I can also serve as a leader in my community, a power partner and sometimes a mentor to others at different points in their own path to success. One thing I always emphasize is that whether you are a corporate executive, entrepreneur, freelance guru-for-hire or employee who may someday face a career change, you are also the manager of your own personal brand, and you will have to be ready to articulate your exceptional skills and value proposition effectively and without warning. This is another common fear, but preparing and practicing ahead of time is key. Expressing your value effectively can have a tremendous impact on your success: it may immediately motivate others to want to know you better, to do business with you, or simply speak highly of you to everyone they know.

I have come to realize, as much as I enjoyed that original compliment about being great at reinventing myself, that we don't have to deliberately set out to make reinvention happen. It is a law of nature that life will reinvent us many times over, whether we ask for it or not. It is our job to be centered and ready with clear priorities, a strong support system and the ability to re-engage the same tools, skills and wisdom that have already made us who we are. It begins with figuring out what it is that gives you faith in yourself, and then learning to say it out loud in a way that reaches out to others.

In the end, my values, choices and relationships are my real identity. Someday, I hope that the wonderful people in my life will come to think of me as a person who successfully reinvented herself and yet didn't really change at all.

## Noël Thelander

Noël Thelander is a financial advisor who emphasizes collaboration and education. She collaborates with her clients' tax and legal professionals, works to help family members collaborate in defining what financial success means to them and guides her clients in taking the appropriate actions to achieve their most serious financial goals.

In addition to advising clients, Noël teaches and coaches them as they consider their particular needs and goals in various stages of life, from their working and education planning years through pre-retirement, retirement and estate transitions. Noël has a gift for translating the complicated language of finance into understandable concepts and for looking out for the best interests of her clients and their loved ones.

Noël is a charter member and Chapter Leader of the DPWN Woodstock, Illinois chapter where she specializes in working with business owners, generations of families and women of all ages who are ready to be more engaged in their family's long term financial strategy. Noël lives in Crystal Lake, Illinois with her husband and two teenage daughters.

Noël Thelander, AAMS™
Financial Advisor
815-353-9416
noel.thelander@ml.com
www.linkedin.com/pub/noel-thelander/24/a49/59a/en

# Noel Baldwin
## *I Can't Wait to See What's Next*

When anyone drives up to my office in Woodstock, IL, they might be surprised that my company name—NBaldwin Company—is the only sign on a large one-story building. I remember the day the sign was hung and the ribbon was cut to open my business in its own building. I looked at my name hanging above the door and thought, "Oh, my gosh, I'm a real business! That's MY name hanging there!"

NBaldwin Company offers accounting and tax services, fraud and forensic services. Reading that, you might think I spend my day poring over spreadsheets, blinking my eyes wearily at closing time after tedious hours with columns of numbers. While there are spreadsheets and columns of numbers in my work, I don't find them boring or tedious. I LOVE accounting— everything about it (well, except writing financial reports). I love analyzing numbers, finding tax savings, helping to put a new business on a solid financial footing, and discovering how to make a business more successful. I love the way my work with these numbers and records helps people organize and maintain their financial lives. The fact that the work I love can help people is the best part of my job.

When I was very young, my girlfriend and I would play at each other's houses. At her house we played with Barbie dolls; at my house we played store or bank. My mother saved coupons and postcards from magazines for me because I loved to fill them out. I guess I always knew someday I'd be doing something involving money and business. I also knew that work was an important part of life and that making money was the way to get the things I wanted. I remember the day I asked my mother if I could buy a dress and she told me we couldn't afford it. I didn't get angry or upset. I just had a sudden realization that I've never forgotten: The only way to have the money you need is to earn it yourself.

My father owned a restaurant, so I had many jobs available there. In fact, it was there that I first learned to balance books and keep accounts for the restaurant. I took business courses in high school and after I graduated began what would turn out to be a lifetime of studying. At first, I went to the local community college, to get an Associate's Degree—course by course as I could afford the time and/or the money for each one. I attended a satellite location of Columbia College-Missouri to complete my Bachelor's Degree in two and a half years while working full time. Subsequent courses for certifications were always followed by grueling exams. I became a Certified Public Accountant, then continued with courses and exams to become a Certified Global Management Accountant and a Certified Information Technology Professional. Each certification has been in response to my hunger to learn more about my field and to bring new expertise to my work for clients. Most recently, I've veered off into a new branch of financial analysis—fraud and forensic services—and am now a Certified Fraud Examiner.

I went to work for a large corporation a few years after high school, starting out as a payroll clerk in the transportation department. The first day, as I was being ushered to my desk, we passed an office door with the title "Controller" on it. "That's it," I told myself. "That's the office I want to have someday." And I got there! I rose in the company to be controller of that department and then even higher, to become a financial analyst for the corporate specialty division.

As time went on, I realized I was becoming more frustrated with the corporate world. I was working long hours and had major responsibilities all for the sake of the corporation. I recognized that I'm really an entrepreneur at heart. What was I doing for my own sake? What work would really bring me satisfaction and personal success? Just at that time the corporation was moving its headquarters out of state and wanted me to move with them. Instead, I quit and began the NBaldwin Company on a prayer, in a shared office and with no clients.

All of the above took a few paragraphs to describe, but it took three decades to live. I married right after high school graduation and am still married to the same man thirty-two years later. We have two sons. I worked full-time the entire time I was raising them and taking classes. So in those paragraphs you can weave in the sleepless nights, the cramming for exams, the meals on-the-run and the late arrivals home that come with trying to balance work life and family life. What you might not weave in I will supply for you now:

**There were pivotal moments in my life that set my direction and influenced me.**

From my earliest years I've been driven by grit and determination. I'm always challenging myself—there's something else to learn; there's some new way to do this—and I'm not happy being sedentary. I believe every moment of life is meant to be lived as fully as possible. I wouldn't be the same person if I hadn't had experiences that stopped me in my tracks and sometimes even turned my world upside down.

When I was seventeen, my twenty-year-old brother and I were both engaged on the same night. So we planned a joint wedding. One month after the engagement, my brother was killed in a car accident. Everything changed in one terrible moment. My family was never the same. My marriage started with us sharing a devastating load. My parents lost their first-born child their only son. We had been a close family; now my sister and I were closer to my parents than ever; my husband became another son.

On the twentieth anniversary of my brother's death, my mother was killed in a head-on collision. Like my brother, she died too young. Her life was cut-off with no warning, and no time to prepare. Six years after my Mom died, with no warning, my Dad passed away peacefully in his sleep. Along with my grief, I found my conviction renewed—don't miss a chance to live. Pay attention to everything and go for what you want to accomplish NOW.

**I rely on significant mentors and support systems.**

I have come to recognize other people's expertise and to trust it and learn from it. Early in my corporate career, the controller became my mentor. He encouraged me when I took on tasks that nobody else wanted so I could learn about the workings of the company. He recognized how well I handled people and how eager I was to learn; and he supported my decision to go to school full time to earn my Bachelor's Degree.

My husband and sons have been my most solid support system all these years. Their patience and understanding while I was going to school full-time and their sincere encouragement as I've aimed for each new milestone have been the bedrock of my success. Furthermore, besides being a support, my husband has been one of my best business mentors. He is a manager and has taught me invaluable management skills and strategies. In the second year of my new accounting business when I had made no money and was thinking about quitting, my husband said, "Give it one more year. See how it goes and if it doesn't get better in the third year, then you should quit." He was right! In my third year, the business turned around and began to see a profit. In the following nine years, it has grown to point that I now have my own office building and will soon hire new associates.

**I look at struggle as an opportunity.**

Nothing comes without effort and sometimes even opposition. Within any of those struggles, I know there are opportunities to learn and change. I try to teach that to my clients, too. I'm a good listener and I'm astute. As I'm looking at someone's personal or business financial troubles, solutions come to me. I'm also good at pointing out strengths and weaknesses in a constructive way.

No client or business has the same needs as another. I'm convinced that my own life experiences have led me to understand people's different money needs and their different levels of understanding.

I believe that in the next few years, I'm going to have two full time assistants and a partner to focus on the tax and business part of the NBaldwin Company, while I focus on fraud and forensics. As always, I'm still asking myself, "What's next?" I can't wait to find out.

## Noel Baldwin

Noel Baldwin, CPA, CFE, CGMA, CITP, is the owner of NBaldwin Company, which offers accounting and tax services as well as fraud, forensics and financial analysis for individuals, trusts, estates, and corporate clients ranging from small to mid-sized businesses.

Noel holds a Bachelor of Science Degree in Accounting from Columbia College, Missouri. She is a Certified Public Accountant of Illinois and a Certified Fraud Examiner. She is a member of the American Institute of Certified Public Accountants, the Illinois CPA Society, the National Association of Certified Valuation Analysts and the Association of Certified Fraud Examiners. She is also a Notary Public of Illinois.

Clients find that Noel takes the time to know their business or personal financial situations and to understand their needs. She tailors the work she does to each client and makes sure that they understand and are satisfied with solutions she offers to meet both long and short-term accounting needs.

Noel Baldwin
NBaldwin Company
330 E Jackson St.
Woodstock, IL 60098
815-206-5647
nbaldwin@baldwincpa.net
www.BaldwinCPA.net

# Jordan Holwell

## *Me Strong?*

Am I strong? And if you think so, why?

That was the question I had to ask.

My friend Jacqueline gave me this amazing opportunity: to be a part of this book. She said it was about "strong" women. I was a bit taken aback, and asked, "Jackie, what makes you think I'm strong?" Her response? "Well, the events in your life, everything you were able to overcome and get to where you are… you have an amazing gift."

Up until this point in my life, I thought I was just living my life. You know, taking the good with the bad, bearing my cross, knowing that God never gives me more than I can handle. However, I was suddenly tasked with understanding my strength. So, I asked others about it.

The responses I got varied from "You rescue animals and provide a safe, loving home for them," to "You're not afraid to speak your mind and stand up for what you believe in." I didn't realize that those are qualities of being strong. I thought it was just who I am.

And who I am has been shaped by many things. Some of them are good and some are bad. Incredible people have come into my life, and profoundly and forever changed me. And certain life events took me down roads that I never thought I'd travel. It's undeniable that some of those people and events left me with some negative thoughts about who I am. I played those "tapes" for far too many years. But at some point, I found faith, and with that faith, I found love, and with love, I found ME and I learned to love me! I was then able to make a difference in my world. But those "tapes" haunted me for a long time, popping up in my head whenever I would begin a new job, friendship, or try to move forward in some way.

I'll share some of the events and people with you….and you'll see one person was with me throughout my journey.

At 18, when I told my mom my plan to finish two years at community college and go to Berkeley and then law school, she said I was too stupid to get into law school and that I should become a secretary. I listened. I had no faith with nothing bigger than myself to believe in. I believed in her, I trusted her.

At 23, I was coerced into going to church with a co-worker, because you see, I was an atheist. Funny thing happens when you share that with people…. they want to convert you. Quite honestly, I got so sick and tired of her bugging me….I told her, "I'll go with you ONE time, and then you have to leave me alone". She agreed and I went. 27 years later I'm still going, and with each day, and each experience, my faith grows exponentially.

At the same time in my life, I worked for a man named Howard Horace. He was a Lieutenant Colonel in the Army and he became my second Dad. He is still on the fringe of my life, and he taught me strength, kicked me in the butt when I needed it; and offered a shoulder and the words I needed on some of the worst days of my life. God was there too, my heavenly Father.

At 26, I lost a child. I didn't see it at the time, but God was in control….

When I turned 29, I became involved in the youth ministry at my church, Trinity Christian Fellowship, for many years. As God would lead, there was a family, the Kims, who came to me at church one day and told me that they so believed in the ministry I was doing, that they wanted to pay for my tuition at Rhema Bible College, where I'd wanted to attend. God spoke and they listened.

Between the ages of 17 and 36, I was in and out of one bad, abusive relationship after another. They were all long-term… so now I joke that at least I had long-lasting relationships. (If you can fix them, you fix your family…

right? NO!!) And who protected me through this, even when I didn't know it? God.

When I was 31, my Mom passed suddenly. Five months later, my sister, and my hero, Kim, was diagnosed with breast cancer. My dad asked me to quit my job and help take care of her, which I did, until her daughters, Brett and Paige, could finish the current semester at college and come home. It was during one of our many discussions that she said, "Jo, promise me that you won't live your life with regrets." And I promised. However, it took me another 12 years before I kept that promise. And God provided strength.

At 32, my sister Kim passed away much too soon and I lost my hero. At this point I was sure that God had left me....but I was wrong...He carried me and provided comfort.

At 33, after offering to give me a small down-payment for my first house, my father told me, three weeks before closing, that he wouldn't give me the money because I'd failed at everything I'd ever done. Though, years later, he didn't recall saying that. I raised the money myself. Guess who provided it.... God.

At 34, I had a massage that would forever change the course of my life. I hadn't seen Alyse, a family friend, in over 25 years. We reconnected when her mother passed away. We stayed in touch, and planned a visit a year later. While I visited with her in Texas, she treated me to a massage, and the woman who did my massage also did CranioSacral Therapy. What happened during that session profoundly changed me forever. I left there knowing one thing: I wanted to learn CranioSacral Therapy. That was a divine appointment from God. But it would take another four years.

Shortly after that, my Dad became ill, and I moved home to help take care of him. I worked nights so that I could be with him during the daytime. And if you've ever had the privilege of taking care of an ailing parent, it is stress that you never realized existed. And God gave patience.

At 37, while working at a fitness center, a member came in who had a certain presence. I just wanted to follow him around and listen to him speak. One day, I finally approached him. We had a discussion that put me on my path to today. He owned a wellness center where he taught CranioSacral Therapy and he invited me to take a class. I did and I was hooked. God showed me how vast He was.

At 40, after 4 years of caring for my Dad, I realized he needed more help than I could provide. Everyone did not agree, and a family battle for power began. Lines were drawn in the sand. It was family dysfunction at its finest. I moved out and found myself, starting over. I began hopping from job to job, hoping that with each move I'd find my passion. Why I thought now would be any different than a lifetime of hopping was beyond me. But God had me on a path. I realize now, that with each new hop, I was getting closer and closer to where God needed me to be.

At this time, I also became an ordained minister. My friend Louise B (may God bless her soul), asked if I was still involved in ministry and if I could perform her niece's wedding. I said that I was involved in ministry, but I couldn't perform the wedding because I wasn't ordained. I explained it's not that easy and that there are steps you have to take. She insisted. I called a pastor that I'd known for many years. We had a lengthy discussion. I had some work to do, but he blessed and ordained me. Now God had my attention.

At 43, one day, I woke up and decided that I was sick of living my life in a 9-to-5 office job that made me hate myself every day. I prayed about it, asking, "God, where am I supposed to be? What am I supposed to do?" Very clearly now, the answer was "Start your own business doing CranioSacral Therapy." I said, "What, I can't do that!" Believe me, it was quite a discussion. BUT, the next day, I walked in and quit my job! I was scared to death! But it was what I was meant to do. God asked me to get out of the boat and trust Him.

At first, I just helped friends, and those I worked on had profound experiences and changes. The more I worked, the more intrigued I became with the human body; and wanted to learn everything I could. After much thought, I decided that the best plan was to attend massage school. But I was 44 years old! How could I possibly do this at my age? Where do I get the money? God said, He'd be right there beside me, and He would provide.

Boy, was I in for a ride. I had never studied biology, anatomy, physiology. Science was not my friend. Several times, those negative tapes played… "You're not smart enough," "You've failed at everything you've ever done…." God told me otherwise. He told me, "You are spectacular, I give you wisdom, and I've given you a gift that the world needs. You will not fail." I had to clear my head, block out the noise and move forward. I studied my ass off and I excelled.

At 45, I became a Licensed Massage Therapist and I have succeeded! I have done what I never thought I could do. I own my own business. I am well respected in my field. I have a fire, and a passion, for helping others that makes getting up each morning a gift. I realize that I did not achieve this on my own. I realize that MY God is the reason I am here.

At some point, you need to take a long look at who and what shapes and defines you. With the help of some amazing people, I began to really take a look deep inside and here's what I learned…..

Did my parents make me question my sanity on more than one occasion?

Yes!

Did I play those negative tapes for many years?

Yes!

Did those tapes send me on a path in my life that included ridiculous choices and feelings of failure and inadequacy?

Yes!

Have I been able to forgive the past and those that hurt me? Including myself?

Yes!

BUT, that's all okay, because as I write this, I have to say that had I NOT taken the path that I did, I probably wouldn't find myself here today.

And today includes happiness.

But most importantly, I've learned, that along with being happy, you are never too old to change, to learn or to remake yourself. Find your faith, be true to it. Let God's spirit manifest itself within the deepest part of your being. I am in no way perfect, and I am certainly not an outstanding Christian. I often say, I'm the most inappropriate Christian you will ever meet. I'm a broken mess! But I know God loves me just the same, and meets me right where I'm at. He thinks that I'm spectacular. And for some weird reason, He chose to use ME in this amazing healing ministry He's entrusted me with. I'm sure that one day, when I am face to face with my Creator, He may not say, "well done good and faithful servant" but simply "I'm glad you made it."

# Jordan Holwell

    Jordan Holwell is a Licensed Massage Therapist and the Owner of Higher Energy Massage Therapy. Jordan is committed to helping clients to improve the quality of their lives from the inside out. She is also committed to educating the masses on the benefits of massage for emotional and physical healing.

    Jordan's own introduction to the benefits of bodywork was what initially gave her the desire to help others. "I had my first CranioSacral session over 12 years ago, and it was that experience that led me to where I am today," she says. "The profound change that happened within, after that one session, left me with a passion for energy and massage work."

    With her new-found enthusiasm, Jordan began taking courses at the Sacred Journey Institute in Tinley Park, studying the principles of CranioSacral Therapy. In 2009, she founded Higher Energy Massage Therapy. However, her education in the field of holistic wellness wouldn't end there.

Jordan, who is a strong advocate of integrative health and wellness practices and natural healing, went on to graduate from the Cortiva Institute of Massage Therapy. Her current practice is as diverse as her varied background, enabling her to bring a combination of CranioSacral Therapy, relaxation and therapeutic massage to the table. "The opportunity to help others facilitate healing is endless," she says.

Jordan Holwell
Higher Energy Massage Therapy
445 West Jackson Ave
Naperville, IL 60540
708-769-5634
jordan@higherenergy.net
www.HigherEnergy.net

# Sabrina Swanson

## *Dreaming in Color*

"Are you Dreaming in Color?" As I went from corporate America to owning my own business, that question was and still is the key to my growth. Why, you ask? Let me answer with a few questions: 1) Have you ever felt that you shouldn't be in business for yourself? 2) Have you ever felt the roller coaster effect in your business? 3) Have you ever thought, am I just not a good business owner? I have no contacts and no one wants what I have to offer? I have felt like that many times. Looking back at those down moments, I forgot my purpose and my dream…in color.

I needed a technique that would always keep my dream and goals in front of me and guide me. That is when I learned about a Dream Board. It is like a genie bottle. I say that since I have done several Dream Boards over the years. When I go to update my Dream Board, I always have to make a fresh one. With my last Dream Board, I achieved everything that I put on the board.

Example #1: I had a picture of a professional female speaker that I admired. I wanted to be like her and have no trouble speaking in front of crowds; to speak and train in confidence. Well, that isn't a problem now. I LOVE speaking and training in front of a crowd.

Example #2: Credit Card debt. I wanted to pay off my husband's and my credit card debt in 3 years. I put a picture of each credit card bill on the Dream Board with a paid in full written on each bill. I am happy to say I will have paid the cards off in 3.5 years.

Example #3: Health. I put a picture of running shoes, gym equipment and new clothes on my dream board. I now work out 2-3 times a week and am more aware of what I eat. I am no longer eating at fast food places 7 days a week.

Example #4 Helping Others. I have numerous pictures for this category since I am able to give back in so many ways because of Dreaming in Color. Volunteer work, community service projects and being on the Board for the Elk Grove Village Lions Club allow me to help hearing and sight impaired individuals near and far, just to name a few things.

To Make a Dream Board:

~Poster Board

~Glue

~Scissors

~Old magazines to cut out COLORED pictures

~Markers

~Bills

~Vacation destination pictures

I always sign my name and date on my Dream Board. I take full ownership. Once I have completed the Dream Board, I place it where I can see it. It is a constant reminder of what I want to achieve. I always add items to the board when I think of additional things. They not only help myself but my family. EXAMPLE: My husband needed a car, so he put a picture of a car on the Dream Board and guess what happened?? Yes, he got a car. I did my first Dream Board by myself. I now include my husband since this affects both our lives in such a great way. Team work and a true partnership.

Once I finish my Dream Board, I use it as a tool to make and implement a plan...a business plan. This plan can be updated as often as I like for the positive growth I need for me both professionally and personally. I start by picking the date(s) that I want to achieve each item on my Dream Board. It includes Month, Day and Year. From that date, I work backwards on each step that I need to do in order to achieve that goal…dream. I do both a best AND a worst case scenario plan. Life happens, so I make sure that I am prepared with my detailed plan. All it takes is one bump in the plan and I start to go off track. A plan and Dream Board usually prevent that from happening. I add daily devotional reading time, play time-such as going to the movies, lunch with the girlfriends and date night. As much as I can add in detail to the business plan, I will be able to dream in BRIGHT and BOLD colors.

Remember the three questions at the beginning of this story? I no longer ask myself if I should be in business for myself, I now ask how I can share and help others with their businesses. I now can catch the roller coaster and put on the brakes when I feel that I am headed downward. I control the roller coaster ride with more balance and no longer second guess what I have to sell or if I am a good business owner. I now focus on always doing my very best for others and building relationships. The rest will follow in place. It is truly a great feeling to be more in tune with upward growth, achieving my goals and the ripple effect that it has on the people in my immediate circle and abroad. There are even times when something happens in my life that wasn't on my Dream Board. That makes my day. Pay it Forward, Karma, Go-Giver really falls into place.

So, when in doubt, remember to "Dream in Color", you are worth it!

# Sabrina Swanson

I came from the cellular industry where I was managing a 2.5 million budget used to implement marketing concepts. Though it was very exciting and I traveled a lot, I wanted to be my own boss. I left the corporate world in 1998 for the world of direct sales. I like that what I put into my business is what I get out of it. It is not just control of the financial freedom for my husband and me. It is also the freedom to be with my husband, family and friends whenever and wherever needed.

You hear the words flexibility, financial freedom and be your own boss many times from a "Direct Sales" individual. If it weren't for Direct Sales, I wouldn't have grown to be the person that I am today. I feel empowered and happy.

I get to share with and offer my fashion directors, hosts and customers the same opportunity I have. In addition to sharing jewelry fashion trends to women with Jewels by Park Lane, I get to build the relationships of a lifetime.

"I get to" is the key phrase. Not I have to.

Sabrina Swanson
Jewels by Park Lane
609 Wellington Ave
Elk Grove Village, IL 60007
847-909-9197
sswansonil@aol.com
www.ParklaneJewelry.com/rep/sswanson

# Carol O'Meara

## *Explore and Dream to Discover Your Strengths: An Australian Story*

"Twenty years from now you will be more disappointed by the things that you didn't do than by the ones you did do. So throw off the bowlines. Sail away from the safe harbor. Catch the trade winds in your sails. Explore. Dream. Discover." Mark Twain

Prior to leaving the comfort of my safe harbor, I thought that being an independent woman with a great job was the American dream. However, if you don't know where you're going and how to get there, how do you know if you're living that dream? I realized that I was stuck. I was without a dream and without direction. I was following the dreams of others within my personal and professional network. While this was comfortable, I needed a vision of my own. I needed to move from feeling 'comfortably numb' to being someone who was strong enough to follow her own dreams.

My dream involved spending more time developing my strengths and less time worrying about the small stuff and the situations that were out of my control. By concentrating on this dream that I thought would never change, my work in the US became more demanding with longer hours spent trying hard to be all that I could be. With long hours came complications, and although this brought success, it was not my dream of happiness. I soon found myself back to where I started, 'comfortably numb' following the dreams of 'Corporate America'.

## An Unexpected Reason to Change

People who know me know that I do not like surprises. Ironically, the happiness that I was seeking came to me in the most unexpected way. I met my future husband. Everything was going well, until one Thursday evening in the carpark of a jazz club, the (#@&!) said he was going back to Australia! Knowing a long-distance relationship was not going to work for me, I had to let him know that if he wanted this girl to be a part of his future, then he'd better put a ring on it before returning to Australia! Well, he was planning to do just that and asked me to marry him. Of course, I said yes to this guy! The next thing that I knew, we were married. He was in Australia and I was in the US preparing for the big move. It never occurred to me the distance of where I was traveling to until someone brought it to my attention. "It takes a strong woman to move way across the other side of the world, to a place that she knows nothing about and has never been, with no job, and leaving all that you know behind! Are you sure you know what you're doing?" I knew what I was doing. However, like any major life change, it can be frightening for some people. Yet, part of me didn't want to know much about Australia prior to my arrival. I knew that I needed to discover her for myself, to feel her strong sunrays on my face, and to ask her to be merciful during my journey. It was that moment when I knew that I'd made the right decision to let go.

All that remained was completing the difficult task of saying goodbye to my family and friends. It also meant selling possessions that could not be shipped like my life size Native American Indian totem pole. After the yard sales, car sales, and the packing 208 boxes for the shipping container, it was time to start my new journey in Australia. I boarded the 24-hour flight from the US alone and slept very little on the flight. I spent most of the time reflecting on the strengths I had found to leave the US. I was bringing my knowledge and education to my new life down- under. During my reflection, I knew I couldn't turn back. I was actually living my dream! As my uncontrollable tears of joy and sadness soaked my face, it was time to push my flight attendant button, order an Australian Shiraz wine, and recline my chair. As the Australians would say, 'You have to roll up your sleeves, and get in to it!'

## Saying Yes to Australia

Saying yes to living in Australia is a lot easier than actually living in Australia. I was thinking that I was going to spend my days patting kangaroos and cuddling koalas! I was expecting a white Christmas, a Sydney skyline and endless sunny days. I was excited to meet my new family, make new friends and to start a business in Australia. This was my chance to reinvent myself and to have a new meaning of work/life balance. This was my time to use all that I had learned to avoid repeating the pattern of following other people's dreams. Nothing was going to stop me now from living my dreams.

Culture shock hit me hard. Once I was in Australia, there came moments when I felt depressed, lost in my travels, alone and afraid. I wondered if I had made the right choice. I wasn't sure if I would fit in. I was speaking the same language but seemed as if I couldn't understand what anyone was saying. I felt like I needed a translator and was embarrassed to keep asking people to repeat words or part of conversations. Eventually, I just gave up. I wasn't sure if I wanted to stay.

## Choosing When to Stay and When to Exit

I decided to stay in Australia. The thing that helped me the most was to think about my transition like the Round About. This circular traffic island described my feeling of going around in circles. A roundabout has entrances and exits. Locals entering and exiting the roundabout have a vision and an exit strategy for getting off the roundabout! For me, it was just the opposite! I was unsure when to enter the circle because:

- I was totally new to the country

- I had no previous experience in Australia

- I had no idea of how to get off of the roundabout

- I didn't know the language (I will talk more about this in a moment)

- I didn't know what side of the road to use

- I didn't know how to start a business

- I was confused about all of the acronyms!

## Stuck in a Roundabout

I was stuck in my roundabout! My emotions were high and I had no vision and no exit strategy. I had knowledge and experience which was valuable in the US but networks, trust and relationships do not transfer to Australia. I had many false starts with businesses with little return. I was trying to start a business without knowing the business. I was spending too much time in my business and not enough time on my business. The defining moment in my transition involved taking time off from my new business and returning back to the States to visit family and friends. This was one of the best mental health choices that I've made in many years. The time off gave my brain a chance to reboot. I prepared to spend some quality time with folks and to share my experience with a new set of eyes. One of my friends invited me back to speak in a class preparing for a semester abroad. During my presentation, I shared with them the following quotation:

"When you travel, remember that a foreign country is not designed to make you comfortable. It is designed to make its own people comfortable."

- Clifton Fadiman

At the end of my presentation, I give them a small koala bear toy and we 'enjoyed' a sample taste of some Vegemite. As I saw the negative reactions to this Australia treat, I suddenly realized what needed to change. In my comfort zone, I was able to realize that the local culture was not designed to make me comfortable, it made the locals comfortable. Armed with this new understanding, I was ready to return to Australia and take on my transition with a new set of eyes.

## Seeing My Challenge as an Opportunity for Growth

When I returned to Australia, I realized that I was not alone in my roundabout. There were different people experiencing the same problem of entering and exiting their roundabout. They had no sense of direction and no strategy for getting off the roundabout. I reached out to a few of these women and formed a monthly book group. While we did not necessarily read books, we always had healthy, long conversations with lots of laughter, shared stories and a bond. Spending more time with other like-minded women gave me the opportunity to talk about my feelings, interests and challenges.

Another solution was the Women's Business Association. As founder, I wanted WBA to enable women to work together to find solutions rather than to continue to be lost as individuals, riding alone in the roundabout without a vision or an exit plan. In other words, having a guide at your side is a quicker way in and out of the roundabout.

**Getting Back into the Groove**

It felt great when I discovered that my vision was becoming my reality. Part of my vision was to increase my leadership skills and role within my business and the community. In my experience, I was taught in the military that a strong leader has to be "front and centred" and must know everything. As you know, this is not accurate. My Australian business depended on bringing in the right people with the right knowledge to service my clients efficiently. I also depended on them to do their job and to consult with me for advice and feedback. My leadership style was democratic not because I wanted to have everyone involved in decision-making but because I welcomed their involvement.

My path towards personal growth involved changing my way of thinking in order to embrace my new country. It was not easy for me. I had to learn a new language and mannerisms. It was not about placing my culture aside and forgetting about it, but moving it to the side to allow me to see clearly what's right in front of me. I had to go through three stages for the dramatic change.

The first was the Ending Stage, where I had to let go of everything I knew that was stable, known and dependable. This ending for me was leaving the US with my family, friends, work and everything. It was starting over.

The second stage was the most difficult in my personal growth and took the longest. This was the Middle/Neutral Zone, where I was forced to hang in mid-air, without orientation to the past or the future. This is my roundabout. I could not get off or did not know when to do so. I did not know what my future in Australia held for me. I was in Australia for about three years, when I felt this way and was not sure how long it would last.

Finally, I was approaching the New Beginning Stage where I needed local mentors and my support system to reassure me that home is where you make it, and Australia can be my home if I allow it to happen. Once I had allowed myself to exhale, I realized what I had to do. By holding on tight to the "Jesus Bar", I sped through and exited the roundabout madly with excitement and a recognized identity!

**How Carol Got Her Groove Back!**

Getting your groove back is a personal journey. Nevertheless, drivers stuck on the shoulder of their roundabout sometimes need a jump start to get moving again. Here are my tips to get you going:

- Return to your Comfort Zone – the best conditions for learning or seeing things differently occur when we are relaxed and in our comfort zone

- Set your Course to Success – over relying on others can leave you stranded

- Narrow your Focus – if you want to be world-class, you have to find your focus; otherwise, you will be busy without achieving much.

- Prepare to Go the Distance - "There are no shortcuts to any place worth going" - Beverly Sills

- Look Up Regularly – while in your zone, take some time to discover your strengths, know where you are, where you're going and where you need to be

- Stop and Ask – accept that others may have the answers to your unanswered questions

- Check your Dashboard – Review your progress and reconnect with people regularly along the way

- Pull Over – people creating lives of significance need a power nap to recharge their battery (working 60 hours at 25% is the same as 15 hours at 100%) to work smarter not harder

- Know When to Get Off – know what success is for you and what it looks like if you go too far

- Take a Second Time Around – avoid mediocrity by being prepared to re-enter the roundabout; it is not always about getting off or out as quickly as possible

These are the tips I am currently using myself and with my clients who are navigating their own roundabouts.

**Returning to a Familiar Harbor**

Plunging head first into the unknown and unknowable of my work, life, and cultural transitions, involved leaving a safe harbor where I had been very comfortable and secure. While I did not know what was ahead, my experiences made me a stronger woman and enabled me to achieve levels of success that I'd never thought possible, especially in another country. My decision to explore and dream allowed me to discover my strengths while living outside of my comfort zone in Australia. Now back in the United States, I'm transitioning again but differently. Even though I experienced a similar process such as packing and selling the house, yard sales, 60 boxes, my Australian businesses are international and I'm still living my dream. I am not the same woman who left for Australia 14 years ago, nor will I ever be. I'm a stronger woman in the driver's seat who now says, "I got this!", rather than, "What is this?" every time I enter life's roundabouts.

I'm no different from you. It takes strength from all corners in your life and energy to enter your roundabout alone to stay long enough to be aware of whom you need to be and what you need to get there. Just tell yourself, "You got this"; and rather than wait for the perfect exit, just take an exit and make it perfect.

Follow your dreams, accept that there will be challenges, and explore all the possibilities that will come your way when you leave the safe harbor of your comfort zone.

# Carol O'Meara

Carol O'Meara [MSM; GradDipCouns; BA (HRM)] is the President of Diverse People Solutions, professional and executive coach, specializing in work, life and culture transitions. Carol is also a US military veteran and a corporate consultant with significant global experience. Her direct experience with achieving her goals during multiple transitions has helped her become an expert transition coach. She uses her life lessons and a strengths-based approach to assist her clients to accelerate their transitions.

Carol drew on her strengths during her own transitions from management positions in the US to a new life and a new career while experiencing the culture shock of living in Australia. Within weeks of arriving, she established DPS and commenced lecturing in Human Resources at Federation University, Australia.

Carol's genuine desire to help others resulted in the referrals that built her business. Her diverse list of clients included representatives from the health, higher education, professional sports, hospitality, government, manufacturing, and transportation sectors.

Committed to inspiring others, Carol encouraged clients to engage in social responsibility programs. Her 'Classroom Connections©', and 'Changing Colours©' programs based in Malawi, drew the attention and support of UNESCO and the Australian government.

While in Australia, Carol formed a non-profit organization for empowering women in regional and rural areas. Events encouraged women to Move Up, Reach Back and Give a Hand Up© to women starting their journey as a business owner. Carol also took time to invest in herself by returning to graduate school and earning a counselling degree.

Back in the United States, Carol has opened a Diverse People Solutions Chicago location and began sharing the secrets of her strengths-based approach when coaching clients to reach their true potential by identifying and applying their unique strengths.

Carol O'Meara
Diverse People Solutions LLC
P.O. Box 992
Arlington Heights, IL 60004
carol.omeara@diversepeoplesolutions.com
www.DiversePeopleSolutions.com

# OVERCOMING *Mediocrity*©

## Volume IV

*Now interviewing authors for our next edition,
scheduled to be released in Spring 2016.*

www.dpwnpublishing.com